Contents

Introduction

Can any book really be *The Only Dog Training Book You'll Ever Need?*

"No way," you're probably thinking—especially if your untrained dog is wreaking complete and utter havoc on your life. Maybe you're pulling out your hair because you have a new puppy who keeps having accidents on your good living room carpet, sinking her razor-sharp baby teeth into you every chance she gets, and chewing through any electronic device, pair of shoes, or purse she can get her eager little mouth on. Or, maybe an older dog who has never been properly trained has just become a member of your family, and you are now desperately trying to undo past damage. No easy task, most likely, if he jumps uncontrollably all over guests, pulls on his leash full force whenever you try to take him for a leisurely stroll, and attempts to dig his way out of the yard with more tenacity than an imprisoned convict. Whatever the specific reasons, the problems that come with training a dog can be overwhelming and exasperating. No wonder you're skeptical!

Try to put your doubts aside, though. Yes, this really is *The Only Dog Training Book You'll Ever Need*. And yes, you really can train even the most unruly canine. But it won't happen overnight. Proper dog training requires serious commitment on your part. You'll never succeed without consistency and constant effort, so be prepared to work hard.

If you're eager to improve your dog's behavior—and you must be, if you're reading this book—you've probably stared at the seemingly limitless range of dog toys and training tools stocked at your local pet store. Perhaps you've sorted through some of them and have found tools you like, but you're not sure you're using them properly. Or, perhaps you've thrown money away hand-over-fist on all sorts of devices, only to be disappointed when they make no difference whatsoever in your dog's behavior. Either way, it's important to remember that these things are just the tools, not the solutions.

When it comes to training, the only *real* solution is you. Yes, admitting that it's all up to you might sound stressful, but think about it. Just as parents are the primary source of guidance and shaping for their children, so are you for your dog. The responsibility is huge, but the end result is infinitely rewarding. The good news is you don't have to rely on all sorts of gadgets, because you do have what it takes. You just need to learn the proper techniques.

The basis for all of the techniques in this book centers around clicker training. As you read through each chapter, you'll learn more about what it is and how it works. The important thing to keep in mind is that with clicker training, yelling, punishing, or forcing will all become obsolete, because the skills you'll learn will enable you to communicate with and teach your dog effectively. These methods aren't temporary solutions—you'll be enabling learning for the long haul.

Start by paying close attention to your dog's personality and habits, being mindful of what causes her to misbehave and then preventing it, and praising and acknowledging the things she does right. Most of all, set yourself up to be the best leader you can be for your dog. If you're serious about learning along with your dog— and building a closer, more rewarding relationship with him while you're at it—gear yourself up and start reading this book now!

1: The Tricks to Good Dog Training

The time you spend training your dog is critical to fostering your relationship with him. It's important to establish a good relationship with your dog from the start, and training a dog is like any other relationship. It's partly about providing your dog with rules and boundaries for what is and isn't acceptable, partly about teaching your dog what is expected of her, and partly about spending time together and learning to enjoy each other's company.

From the moment you bring your new puppy home, she is learning how to get along with your family—a species entirely different from her own. Remember, an untrained dog still learns things, just not necessarily the things you want her to know. As I often tell my students, you get what you reinforce. If you don't give her any instruction, or you're vague and inconsistent when you do instruct her, she's sure to get confused, and this confusion will result in undesirable behavior and mischief. But if you pay attention to what your dog is doing right and spend time teaching her what is expected of her, you will be rewarded with a well-mannered pet who becomes a beloved member of your family.

Much of your dog's training has to do with the structure you provide for her regarding what is and is not allowed. Teaching your dog the basics in the midst of various distractions and in new environments is part of being a good dog owner and will help you avoid future behavior problems. The better trained your dog is, the better relationship the two of you will share.

Good training strengthens your bond with your dog, because when you are training him, you are teaching him to share a common language of words and signals. Teaching your dog the meaning of the basic obedience commands gives you a vocabulary for communicating effectively with your dog in day-to-day interactions. As with any communication, you and your dog need to understand each other, and when you do, you'll be amazed at just how intelligent dogs are and what can be accomplished through training. Once you learn to communicate effectively with your dog through training, you can nip behavior problems in the bud and even avoid them altogether.

► **Boston Terrier lounges on her bed**

Dogs who are trained to respond to basic commands are fun to own because you can direct their behavior in appropriate ways so that you will have a more enjoyable life together. The strong bonds developed through training will carry over in play and in all other things you do with your dog. If your dog likes to swim and you like to walk on the beach, for instance, think of how much more you'll enjoy your time together if, when the walk is over, you can simply call your dog and he comes right to you.

Training your dog is a lifelong process. The more you practice the skills of a good trainer, the better you'll be, and the more quickly your dog will learn. Once you find a method that works for you, don't change it—you'll confuse your dog and frustrate yourself.

Who Should Train the Dog?

Since dogs thrive on consistency, ideally one person should be the trainer. But dogs who are family pets can adapt well to a multiple-trainer system and feel a special connection to everyone who works with them. However, if family members aren't committed to learning the proper skills, agreeing on rules, and working consistently with the puppy, the person with the most interest should take responsibility.

Charting Your Dog's Progress

The most difficult part of being a beginner is that you are also learning while you're trying to teach your dog. Be patient with yourself—dog training is a physical skill that requires lots of practice and repetition. To train your dog successfully, you need to be able to break things down into component steps that are easily achieved in a training session. It takes time, but there are several things you can do to help speed up the process.

1. Keep a notebook to record your training sessions.
2. Before you begin, map out the steps involved in teaching a particular command.
3. Make sure your plan is flexible, and be ready to add in more detailed steps if your dog has trouble understanding what you want.
4. Arm yourself with the best treats and rewards to keep your dog motivated.
5. Time your sessions—don't go longer than five minutes.
6. Use clicker training consistently to mark and reinforce good behavior: Read the details in Chapter 3 and be sure to familiarize yourself with how it works; it will save you tons of time in the long run.
7. Try to stick to the plan you've mapped out; don't click the dog for lots of different behaviors in one session.
8. If you get stuck on one particular trick, brainstorm with a friend about how to help your dog through it.
9. Add in distractions as soon as the dog starts to get the hang of what you're trying to teach.
10. Don't be afraid to backtrack and review previous steps if your dog's behavior falls apart in a new place.

In general, your dog's attitude is the best measure of your success as a trainer. If you keep sessions upbeat and fun, make it easy for your dog to succeed, and remember to end on a positive note, it won't be long before your dog thinks that working with you is better than anything else in the world.

Consistency Is Key

Practicing on a regular basis is important if you want to become a good trainer and accomplish the goals you've established for your dog. Success will come more easily if you designate several practice times a week. This will ensure that you will have lots of opportunities to experiment with techniques, and your dog will have lots of time to get the hang of working with you. Once you consistently include training in your weekly routine (or daily routine, if your dog is young and learning the basics of living politely with humans), you will realize how easy the whole process is. You'll also appreciate how much fun it is to have a dog that works with you because she enjoys it.

The more practice you put into training your dog, the more creative you'll be with fixing behavior problems. If you take the time to evaluate why your dog is doing what she is doing, you'll find unique solutions that work for you. Getting an idea of "who" your dog is can help you design a training program that will be effective in teaching her to fit in with your family. Finding out how your dog responds to distractions and whether she's motivated by toys or games, for example, might be helpful in putting together a training program that is easy to implement.

How Well Do You Know Your Dog?

Breaking your training sessions down into small steps, learning what motivates your dog, and finding out where your dog is most distracted will help you know where to start. Below are some questions to ask yourself before you begin your training program.

- Is the dog energetic or laid back?
- Does he do something that you've always meant to put on cue but didn't know how to?
- Is his attention span short or long? How does he respond amid distractions?
- What is his favorite treat or toy?
- Does he give up easily or does he persist until he gets the job done?

Understanding your dog's personality and learning style is essential to enjoyable and successful training. Recognizing your dog's individual tendencies and finding just the right treats, toys, and games to grab his attention will help your dog to associate training with fun and help you to achieve your training goals.

Energy Level

Some dogs are couch potatoes; others run circles around us all day. Differences in breed, temperament, and personality all come into play when designing a successful training program. Living with your dog makes you the expert when it comes to knowing her personality and what will work for her. Paying attention to how active your dog is can help you learn about her personality and help you choose a routine that will be easy and enjoyable to teach.

Training Energetic Dogs

Most people who own an energetic dog complain at some point about the dog's lack of self-control. Dogs don't just grow out of this, or wake up suddenly one day and behave better, they must be properly trained. If you don't put the effort into teaching your dog better manners, you will live with a whirling dervish who never learns to hang out and relax with people.

Good training is especially productive in this case, because it requires a certain level of control on the dog's part. She has to focus her attention on your cues and look for feedback on what's going right. Dogs who are constantly on the move need skilled trainers who give them lots of feedback and break exercises down into gradual steps. High-energy dogs get overstimulated easily, and do best in short, concise training sessions with clear goals. Trying to push active dogs too far too fast will result in frustration for both dog and trainer. Teaching your dog should always be fun—if you don't push a high-energy dog to work for long periods, they will love learning new things.

Motivating Less Active Dogs

Lower-energy dogs can be harder to get moving until they figure out what you want. These dogs are thinkers, and they like to know where you're going with all of your instruction. Go slowly if you have a less active dog. Also try to keep your sessions short, because these dogs bore easily and hate repeating things too many times. Training before a meal (using unique treats as rewards) often perks them up and sparks a good session.

Medium-energy dogs are the easiest to work with because they are cooperative even if you make a lot of mistakes and are a bit less organized. They don't mind repeating things over and over, and they are patient with you when you slip up or haven't planned out what you are trying to teach. Dogs with moderate energy levels are laid back and fun; they turn their energy on like a rocket booster when they need to, but generally they're glad to go along with whatever you're doing.

Personality and Social Temperament

Before you begin training, ask yourself some questions about your dog's personality traits. It can save a lot of time if you start training your dog in an environment that isn't so distracting that he can't pay attention. Teaching your dog where he is most relaxed and least distracted, or worried, will help him to be successful.

Dogs who are easily distracted because of their friendliness around people benefit from training sessions that start somewhere quiet, then quickly move on to involve the distractions they find hard to resist. Training your dog to be obedient even in the midst of distractions is one way to ensure that she will listen to your instruction when other people are around.

Shy dogs, on the other hand, are sometimes hard to train in public until they are more confident. With this type of dog, practice in a comfortable environment first, and then gradually integrate distractions with familiar people. The ultimate goal is to incorporate strangers and new places so that your dog will be obedient anywhere.

How Long Will Training Take?

Everyone's idea of what constitutes a trained dog varies. If your definition includes teaching your dog to obey commands such as Heel, Sit, Down, Stay, and Come, around distractions, the answer depends on how quickly you learn basic training skills. If you are willing to devote twenty or twenty-five minutes of daily practice for ten weeks, you and your dog are likely to achieve excellent results. If you've trained other dogs, keep in mind that dogs, like people, have different aptitudes. Just as some people have a facility for language, while others have an inclination for science, some dogs might be better at stays, while others catch on quickly to recalls. Some dogs respond to formal training easily and naturally. Others have a harder time. No matter the initial aptitude, formal training is recommended for all dogs and is most beneficial for those confounded by it. All dogs do learn how to learn, so that after ten weeks, it becomes difficult to separate the naturals from the initially confused or resistant.

What Motivates Your Pooch?

Learning what rewards your dog likes is crucial to being a successful trainer. The reward is your dog's paycheck for playing this training game with you. It has to be something he's willing to work for, not simply something you want him to have. Some people have hang-ups about using food to train dogs. They think it cheapens their bond with the dog. They believe the dog should perform out of respect or love for them. Nonsense. Using food to train your dog gets you where you want to go. Training a dog with what he wants as a reward is respectful to his doggy-ness and effective in the interest of time and resources.

Dogs don't perform out of love; their behavior or misbehavior has nothing to do with their love for us. Even dogs who chew the couch and bite the postman love their owners. But if you want that postman-biter to like your mail carrier, it'll probably take more than just a pat on the head as a reward to get him to cooperate.

Dogs are motivated by and will work for food, just like people work for money. We all need money to pay our bills and live our lives; dogs need food to live and enjoy theirs. Many dogs eat out of a bowl once or twice a day for free. Why not take that food and use it as a tool to train them to behave in an acceptable way? Once a dog is hooked on training and you have a good bond with her, you can use other rewards to reinforce positive, appropriate behavior. Here are some yummy ideas for treats:

- Boiled chicken
- Boiled hamburger
- Popcorn
- Tortellini or other types of pasta (cooked)
- Bread (bagel pieces work great)
- Carrots
- Bananas
- Dried fruit
- Cheerios or other types of cereal

- Freeze-dried liver (found in pet stores and supply catalogs)
- Hot dogs (cooked)

Tips on Treats

When it comes to rewards, people are often surprised to learn that dog cookies and dry dog food don't always cut it. Be creative with rewards—just be sure to keep the pieces tiny if you're using food. Even a Great Dane shouldn't get a treat larger than ¼ inch. Using tiny treats will ensure that you'll be able to train for a longer period of time, because your dog won't get full too fast. It will also minimize calories, so he doesn't exceed his daily requirement. After an extra-long training session with extra treats, remember to cut back a bit on his daily ration of food.

To prevent your dog from getting diarrhea, don't give too much of any one thing. As your dog starts to like the training game, mix in less desirable treats (like dog food) with the yummy stuff so that he never knows what he's getting. Random reinforcement will keep him more interested in the game, and let you accomplish more in each training session.

Other Rewards

Most of the time food rewards are used in training because they are quick and easy. But toys and games are an entirely different category of rewards that your dog might also find exciting. If your dog goes nuts over tennis balls or stuffed toys, or he likes Frisbees or chasing a flashlight beam, you can also use these as rewards, paired with the click (see Chapter 3).

For dogs who like games and toys, make training sessions more exciting by mixing them in with food rewards. Some sessions can be all food rewards, while others are all toys and games, or you can mix it up and see what elicits the best response. When using toys as a reward, make the play part brief and fun. The game might last five to ten seconds, and then the toy gets hidden and you get back to work. That way the reward doesn't distract the dog from the lesson. Here are some ideas for nonfood rewards:

- Playing a short game of fetch, tug of war, or catch
- Hiding a toy and finding it together
- Tossing a Frisbee
- Chasing a stream of bubbles
- Giving lots of happy praise and talk
- Petting your dog vigorously
- Playing "flashlight tag" (have your dog chase the light beam)
- Giving your dog a stuffed dog toy that makes noise

Dogs are affectionate animals, and anytime you spend praising them and showering them with attention is time well spent. Chances are, you'll get as much from the affection and exercise as they do!

Help Your Dog Like other Rewards

Some dogs love toys and will happily work for a toss of the ball—at least part of the time. But even dogs who aren't as crazy about toys can learn to like them if you work at it. It is worth the effort on your part to get your dog interested in varied rewards, because the more he finds rewarding the easier and more effective your training will be. Here's how to get started:

1. Hold your dog on a leash and tease him with a toy.
2. Throw the toy out of range then ignore his struggle toward it, but don't let him get it.

3. Use a helper to make the toy more exciting if necessary.
4. Wait patiently until the dog looks away from the toy and back at you.
5. Mark that moment with a click and allow him to play with the toy as the reward.
6. Back up slowly to increase the distance between the dog and the toy if he doesn't turn away from the toy in about thirty seconds. Click and release him to get the toy when your dog looks back at you.
7. Repeat this with different toys and allow the dog to go play with the helper every once in a while.
8. Keep the play part of the reward brief—about ten seconds.

Warming a dog up like this is a great way to start a training session—it helps the dog realize that it's time to work.

Exciting rewards are critical to an effective program. If your dog isn't turning himself inside out for the reward, find something he likes better. For dogs who have tons of toys but only play with a few, consider grouping them in sets of ten and rotating them each week to keep things interesting. But don't sweat it if you just can't get your dog interested in toys; remember, there's no crime in making your dog work for his food!

Random Reinforcement

Once your dog starts mastering certain behaviors, start giving him treats sporadically. He won't know for sure when he's getting a reward, but he probably won't take the chance on missing one, either.

Reward or Bribe?

Many people complain that in the absence of food enticements their dog won't respond to commands. If done correctly, however, you won't need to use food to prompt your dog to obey. There is a critical difference between a reward and a bribe. A bribe is something that elicits a certain behavior by enticing the dog. For example, your dog is out in the yard and won't come in, so you shake a box of cookies to lure him. This isn't really a bad thing, but it isn't training either. Bribing can have its benefits, however, when you are in a hurry and out of options.

A reward, on the other hand, occurs only after a behavior happens. A reward reinforces the likelihood that the behavior will happen again. For instance, you call your dog at the park and he comes to you; you offer a treat and release him back to play again. A rewarded dog is more likely to come to you the next time you call than a dog who is just leashed and then put in the car to go home. There are two types of rewards at work here: the food reward, which reinforced the dog for coming back; and the consequence for coming back, which is the dog getting to go play again.

The Benefits of Strong Leadership

Dogs are pack animals who thrive on rules, consistency, and expectations. Setting limits about what is allowed and how you expect them to act is not only fair, it's essential to having a healthy, well-adjusted dog. Don't worry! Being a strong, fair leader is not about being physical with your dog. A true leader would never need to pin a dog down or give a harsh correction.

Leadership isn't about forcing dogs to obey. It requires you to provide structure and establish boundaries by controlling resources. The more time you spend establishing yourself as the greatest person in your dog's life—the one who has the ability to give your dog access to everything that is important to him—the more control you will have over your dog's behavior, and the better behaved he will be. Being a strong leader is the first step toward ridding your dog of behavior problems. Following are some guidelines on how to be a strong, fair leader. (The specifics of training these basic commands will be discussed in Chapter 4.)

1. Nothing in life is free. Make sure you give your dog a job. Teach her to Sit for dinner, Lie Down before doors are opened for her, etc.

2. Humans go first through doorways and up and down stairs. This prevents your dog from escaping out the front door or knocking you down the stairs. Teach your dog to Sit and Stay until he is released through the door.

3. Down/Stay sessions for five to twenty minutes at a time help teach your dog self-control and give her a constructive job to perform around distractions and company.

4. No dogs on the beds or furniture. Young dogs should sleep in a crate or in their own bed, not in bed with you. Your bed is the highest, most special place in the house and should be reserved for you only.

5. Don't repeat a command more than once. If your dog doesn't respond on the first try, he does not get what you were offering.

6. Ignore your dog if she nudges you for attention. Leaders give attention on their own terms, not when their dogs demand it.

7. Ignore your dog if he is constantly pushing toys at you. Leaders initiate play and decide when the game starts and ends. This keeps a dog on his toes because he never knows when the fun begins.

8. Follow through. If you've asked your dog to do something

but she does not respond, make sure you help her to get into the right position rather than repeating the command.

9. Provide consequences. Ignore what you don't like; avoid yelling at your dog for barking or jumping, for instance. From your dog's perspective, any attention is better than none, and speaking to the dog can often be mistaken for reinforcement.

Because you control the things your dog wants access to, your leadership will help you build a strong bond with your dog, convincing him that you are the key to everything he desires. Strong leadership will give you the foundation you need to teach your dog how to behave appropriately and become a welcomed member of the family.

Ten Keys to Training Success

Throughout this book, you will learn effective techniques to ensure the success of you as a trainer, and your dog as a student. Most "keys to success" are universal, but it will be helpful for you to think of them in terms of your pet's distinct personality.

1. Be patient. All dogs learn at different speeds and often don't grasp concepts as quickly as we think they should. Having patience with your dog will help him to be successful.
2. Plan ahead. Set your dog up to succeed. If your dog isn't "getting it," the behavior probably needs to be broken down into smaller steps.
3. Be realistic. Don't expect your dog to perform a behavior in an environment you haven't taught him in.
4. Be kind. Use positive methods to teach your dog what's expected of him.

5. Avoid punishment. Harsh corrections have no place in the learning phase of a dog's development. Instead, teach your dog what you want him to do.

6. Reward effectively. Reinforce proper behavior with what motivates your dog. A pat on the head is nice but not necessarily what he wants. Remember that this is his paycheck: Pay up!

7. Be generous. All new trainers tend to be cheap with rewards. Reward correct responses often and don't be afraid to reward exceptionally good responses with extra treats, praise, toys, and love.

8. Set goals. If you don't know where you are going and have not planned out the session, how will you know when your dog's got it?

9. Practice often. Teach your dog in short, frequent sessions.

10. Stay positive. Quit with your dog wanting more. An enthusiastic student is always an eager learner.

If you know your dog well, you will be able to choose training methods that work for both of you. Spend some time with your dog over the next few days and make notes on his energy level, personality, special talents, limitations, and motivations. You might be surprised to learn that he doesn't necessarily like or respond to all the things you assumed he would. Adjusting your teaching style and training sessions can have a profound impact on the success of your training program.

The simple truth of training dogs is that you get what you pay attention to. Set your dog up to succeed, limit his options, and reinforce what's going right. Soon you'll have a well-behaved dog that everyone loves to have around.

2: Meeting Your Dog's Needs

Before you can begin a successful training routine, you need to make sure you've covered all of the basic bases with your dog. All animals have a need for food, water, and shelter, and we provide these things for our dogs with barely a second thought. The often overlooked needs that can mean the difference between a problem dog and a really great dog who is cooperative and well-trained are exercise and mental stimulation. If a dog's needs for exercise, training, and attention are met and she is carefully managed according to her age and training level, you will have fewer behavioral problems and less to correct.

Getting Your Dog Moving

Exercise is a crucial element in any training program, and without enough of it, no real learning will occur. A dog without enough exercise is like a child without recess. What adult would like to teach a math lesson to a classroom full of six-year-old boys who haven't been outside to play all day? Without exercise, your dog will be hard to teach because he just can't be still long enough to pay attention.

Dogs vary in their exercise requirements, but all need at least thirty to sixty minutes of running, playing, and interaction with you or other dogs each day. The amount and type of exercise is dependent upon your dog's overall energy level. A Border Collie or energetic young Lab will need one to two hours of flat-out running and active play, while a couch potato Pekingese might only need a thirty-minute romp. Yet, every dog is different, regardless of the breed and its stereotype. Ultimately, the proper amount of exercise is whatever it takes to make your dog tired enough to be able to exist in your home as a calm, relaxed member of the family. Following are some clues that your dog isn't getting enough exercise:

- She paces from room to room in the house.
- She hardly ever lies down, even when everyone else is relaxed.
- She whines excessively for no apparent reason.
- She barks excessively, sometimes over nothing.
- She digs, destroys, and chews everything in sight.
- She never stops jumping when there are people around.
- She runs away every chance she gets.
- She runs along the fence using any excuse to bark at passersby.

If your dog exhibits some or all of these symptoms, she could probably use more exercise and mental stimulation. Most people don't realize that leaving their dogs in the backyard for hours at a time is not a good way to burn off energy and not nearly enough exercise to relax them. Most dogs, when left to their own devices, don't do anything but bark, dig, or lay around.

If you're going to use your yard as a way to exercise your dog, you will need to go out with her and play games to burn off even a tenth of the energy she's got bottled up. In case you don't have a lot of time during the day to play with your pup, sign up for doggie day care, or hire a pet sitter to exercise your dog while you're at work so that when you come home you can concentrate on training your dog and have a willing student who is ready to work. Inviting neighbor dogs over to play, if your dog gets along with them, might be another option. Any way you look at it, all-out running, chasing, and wrestling is what a dog needs to do in order to be tired enough to be a good pet.

Meet and Greet
Concentrate on socializing your dog to a variety of people, places, and things while he is young. As you familiarize your dog with people, make sure he gets plenty of experiences with both genders and a variety of races and ages. Let him get to know other animals—dogs, cats, horses, goats, birds, guinea pigs, and lizards. Go to the park, a parade, the beach, or an outside shopping center. And occasionally leave your puppy in the care of a trustworthy, levelheaded friend, to teach him to be self-assured in your absence.

Working out Together

For dog owners with an active lifestyle, there are lots of ways a healthy, lively dog can burn off energy while accompanying you. Jogging, mountain biking, and Rollerblading are excellent ways to exercise dogs with boundless energy. Just make sure that you start off slowly and gradually build the distance. Also, pay attention to your dog's feet, checking them frequently for cuts and scrapes. Try to have him run on a variety of surfaces, since pavement is hard on a dog's joints and bones.

Dogs who participate in such activities should be at least one year old and recently checked by their veterinarian for potential health problems. (Just like with people, vigorous exercise can exacerbate certain bone and joint disorders.) A fit dog is happy, focused, and more likely to participate in activities for longer periods of time and without injury.

Watch for Injuries

If your dog refuses to assume a certain position when you're training, don't be afraid to have her checked for an injury. Dogs are stoic animals and rarely show discomfort unless it's obvious. Hiding injuries is instinctive, stemming from their wolf cousins who live by the rule of survival of the fittest.

Games Dogs Play

Games are a great way to boost your dog's interest in learning new things and strengthen your bond with him at the same time. Keep the rules simple and easy to follow, and play often. Involve as many people in the family as you can, and see how much you'll enjoy learning new ways of interacting together. Consider any of the following activities and games:

- **Play fetch**—a great way to tire out a tireless retriever. Use a tennis racquet to hit the ball even farther for all-out sprints.
- **Go swimming**—another excellent activity for a very active dog. Combine it with some retrieving for a really exhausting workout.
- **Play hide-and-seek**—an indoor rainy-day game might provide some dogs with enough activity to relax them for the rest of the day. Also use this game to perk up your dog's recall and teach him that coming to you is always the best option.
- **Hide your dog's toys**—he'll learn to use his nose to track things down *and* bring them back to you.

- **Practice Pavlov**—set up a treat-dispensing toy, and show your dog how to interact with it until it pays off.

Whatever game you play, be sure to have a blast with your dog! Keep the pace fast and interesting, and you will see your dog perk up at the mere mention of playtime with you.

Providing the Right Foundation for Learning

Mental stimulation is the second-most overlooked need of problem dogs. All dogs, regardless of breed or energy level, are intelligent and interactive creatures who love new experiences. Learning new things and solving problems makes life interesting and gives smart dogs something to do. It keeps them out of trouble, too!

Dogs who are tied outside, constantly frustrated, and emotionally neglected might start off friendly and welcoming, but eventually they become aggressive and wary of strangers. They have nothing to do, nothing to think about, no companionship, and are absolutely bored. Dogs like this, even early in their adult lives (two to three years old), are hard to train. They aren't stupid or uncooperative, they're just blank. They simply do not know how to learn.

Lack of early stimulation and training makes it more difficult to teach any animal at a later date, because he has no basis for learning and doesn't quite know what to make of the attention. It is possible to teach these dogs, but it takes extra patience, repetition, and practice. The training techniques and tools described in subsequent chapters will help you teach your dog anything you care to take the time to teach.

It's Never Too Soon to Start: Socializing Young Puppies

If you've just brought home a puppy, congratulations on this great addition to your family. Make sure you show him off—not for your sake, but for his. Begin teaching and socializing your puppy as early as eight weeks of age if he is properly vaccinated and your veterinarian has confirmed his good health. Socialization is an important process, and when it's neglected, puppies never reach their potential. They're less adaptable, harder to live with, and less happy. A dog who's received frequent, early socialization thrives on environment changes, interactions, and training. He is also more likely to tolerate situations he's accidentally, and unfortunately, exposed to—such as kisses from a pushy visitor or a Big Wheel riding over his tail.

Start by providing a safe environment for your puppy to explore. No matter what you're socializing your puppy to, always approach it in a relaxed manner so he will learn to be comfortable and confident when encountering new things. Avoid any experiences that could be intimidating to a young pup, and keep your dog leashed in unpredictable or potentially unsafe situations. This way, you can prevent a wobbly youngster from trying to pick him up, or keep him off the sidewalk as a skateboard zips by.

▶ **Lab mix with ball**

Don't Be Afraid to Try

You should never use any training method that makes you feel uncomfortable because you think it might hurt your dog. However, if you're positive a technique won't do any harm, but you're just not sure if it will work, go ahead and try it to see for yourself. Your dog will benefit greatly from having an owner who is not afraid to try new techniques and is committed to finding the best way possible to train him to be the best companion he can be.

Teach Your Dog to Think

Using the methods in this book will teach your dog how to think and solve problems, which is important for any dog. The techniques are commonly referred to as "clicker training," and are based in proven scientific theory. The rules and guidelines (see Chapter 3) will show you how to use this method to teach your dog anything physically possible. It is so exciting to see a dog grasp the concept of what you are trying to accomplish, and respond well without needing any corrections!

All puppies should attend a well-run puppy kindergarten class that teaches basic commands (Sit, Down, Stay, Come), how to walk without pulling, and how to come when called. The class should also offer playtime for dogs eight to eighteen weeks, and be staff-supervised so everyone has a good experience. It is crucial to the normal social development of your dog that she gets to play with other puppies and safe, well-socialized adult dogs on a regular basis. The more good experiences your young puppy has the easier it will be to teach her anything later in life.

Here's a list of qualities to look for in your dog-training school:

- A limited class size with an instructor/assistant-to-student ratio of 1:6 is ideal.
- The age range of the puppies accepted should be no older than eighteen weeks.
- Handouts or homework sheets to explain exercises are important so that lessons can be shared among family members.
- The whole family should be welcome to attend. (If you include your children, make sure you bring along another adult to supervise them while you focus on training the dog.)
- All training methods should be positively based and use clicker training, ideally.
- Demonstrations should be given with untrained dogs to show the progression of exercises.
- Volunteers or assistants who help with the management of the class should be available to ensure that you get the help you need.

Especially if you find it difficult to block out a specific time for training, enrolling in a group class will motivate you to practice consistently with your dog. In addition to obedience classes, many schools also offer agility classes, tricks classes, fly ball, tracking, hunting, herding, and other types of dog sports, so once your dog has mastered the basics, you'll have plenty of opportunities to move on to more advanced training.

Quick Fix: Work in a Group

Taking a group obedience class can be especially great for dogs who have trouble concentrating on training. The distraction of other dogs will help your dog to realize that she must learn to pay close attention to you. Make sure the ratio of teachers to students is high in your class; twelve students to two instructors is ideal.

Learning something new is more fun when you have the right tools and support—so be sure that the training school's philosophy matches your own and that you feel comfortable there. The best judge of a good puppy kindergarten, or any obedience class for that matter, is you. Ask if you can observe a class before signing up your puppy. Make sure the methods taught are kind and gentle, and that the puppies seem to be getting it. Go on your gut instinct—if you like the instructor and she seems like a person you can learn from, sign up. Train your dog; it's the nicest way to say you love him!

Practice Makes Perfect

As with anything in which you want to excel, the more you practice the better at it you will become. All training is a learned skill; the more you work with your dog, the more effective you'll be as a trainer and as a team. For example, the beginning trainer's timing often needs some work. Through lots of practice, you will find and develop your own training style, discovering what works for you and expanding upon it.

There are tons of books and online resources that will tell you everything you'll ever want to know about dog behavior and training. Search for obedience classes in your area and keep at it. Remember, you and your dog are going to be together for a long time—if you're lucky ten to twelve years or longer. Time spent teaching her how to learn will benefit both of you for years to come. Start your dog on the road to higher learning today!

3: Teaching Without Punishing

Training your dog to behave properly is an ongoing process that constantly requires you to prevent, interrupt, and redirect your dog's less-than-stellar behavior. As humans, we are absolutely convinced that in order to change behavior we must provide punishment to eliminate bad habits. In truth, no animals, including humans, respond well to punishment. Although it has been part of training dogs for decades, punishment is not a good or effective way to train a well-behaved family pet.

The Problem with Punishment

Over time, many trainers have found that it is totally unnecessary to use punishment to prompt reliable, acceptable behavior. In many cases, using punishment can actually make some problems worse. Consider these two points:

- Punishment stops behavior, but it does not teach or provide another choice.
- The many negative side effects of punishment outweigh the short-term benefits.

The best human example of why punishment is ineffective is a speeding ticket. If you've ever been pulled over for speeding, you'll understand. The moment when the lights flash behind you is horrible. Your heart races, you stammer, and then you wait and wait for the police officer to deliver the ticket. Now you've got a fine to pay, and points on your insurance. Do you stop speeding? For a little while you might, but wait until the next day you're running late—you're back to speeding again, and you get away with it.

You were probably a little more careful this next time, but you were speeding. After being punished severely only weeks before, how could you go back to that behavior? Quite simply, the punishment made you a better speeder! You are no longer a random, careless speeder; you actually look for cruisers and avoid known speed traps. The punishment improved the way you speed.

Punishment Is Reactive

The first problem with punishment is that it is a response to bad behavior, whereas training initiates good behavior. The second problem with punishment as a training tool is that you can't always control what the student learns. Punishment is not effective for fixing behavior problems because it is only part of the equation. It stops the unwanted behavior, but it does not show the dog what he should have done instead. Plus, by the time punishment is delivered it is too late to teach the dog anything, because he has already done something undesirable, and it can't be undone.

Punishing your dog for jumping on the company will not make him want to sit in front of them the next time. In fact, punishment delivered by a visitor or in the presence of one might actually teach your dog to be fearful of visitors because it's sometimes unpleasant to be around them. This is not what you want to teach your dog. After all the work you put into encouraging your dog to be social around people, punishing him for being friendly could be detrimental.

Timing Is Everything

For punishment to mean anything, the timing of the correction has to be precise; it must happen the moment the undesirable behavior begins. Not many people, especially average pet owners, are capable of doing this. But even if you were able to respond immediately, usually at the time of the correction the dog is overstimulated and excited, which means her brain is not in learning mode. In order to process information a dog has to be in a fairly relaxed state.

If the timing of the correction were perfect, the dog would need to be rewarded as soon as the inappropriate behavior stopped, because the timing of the reward is the instructive part. When trying to fix a behavior the dog has been practicing for a long time, a very high rate of reinforcement for the right behavior must be employed. Otherwise, the new, desirable behavior will not replace the old behavior. Remember that old habits die hard, and it is difficult to adopt new ways of doing things without being heavily reinforced for the right choices.

▶ **Boston Terrier targeting a target stick**

Redirecting the Behavior

Instead of using corrections, at the first sign of alert or tension, either interrupt the dog or redirect his attention appropriately. You can say the dog's name, touch the dog on the shoulder, or turn away from whatever captured the dog's interest.

To work effectively, interruptions must be delivered before the dog starts the behavior. In the case of barking, for instance, if you wait until the dog is loud and frantic you will not be able to distract him from what he's barking at in order to teach him anything. Even a strong correction wouldn't faze some one-track minded dogs. This is like trying to reason with a person who is angry. When someone is in an irrational frame of mind, they just aren't capable of listening or being reasonable.

Dealing with Distractions

Repeating a command when a dog is obviously too distracted to hear what you are saying is not teaching the dog anything but how to ignore you. The best way to help a dog whose behavior falls apart in a new environment is to go back to kindergarten. Help the dog perform the behavior with a treat or toy as a lure. Drill the dog for five to ten repetitions to get him working again, and then wean him off the extra help. With a little patience and practice, it won't be long before your dog understands that his training works everywhere, regardless of the distraction.

Start paying attention to what triggers the barking, and interrupt the dog while he's still thinking about it. To short-circuit an undesirable behavior, you might have the dog go to his bed, or move further away from the distractions so he's not as excited.

Eventually, your goal is to interrupt him close to the distractions in the environments where the undesirable behavior occurs, but it is unreasonable to train him there in the beginning. As with any constructive and lasting training, you need to start with small, simple steps that enable the dog to be successful.

Establishing New Patterns

In order to stop unwanted behavior and teach your dog new habits, you must have a set plan to accomplish your goal, and you must prevent the dog from practicing the old behavior while you are retraining her. Setting up a new pattern of behavior isn't easy for dogs, because they get into habits like we do and tend to do things the same way again and again if we let them.

Repetition

The important thing to remember when changing a pattern is that you need to practice the new pattern over and over and reward the dog repeatedly for the new behavior until she adopts it as her own. In the meantime, if you want to get where you are going faster, you need to stop allowing the dog to reinforce herself for the wrong behavior by preventing it from happening. Stepping on the leash to prevent jumping will not, by itself, teach your dog to sit, but it will reduce her options and make sitting more likely, because that is the only behavior getting rewarded.

An ounce of Prevention

The more time you spend with dogs, the more you will find that management is a large part of training. Gates, crates, and pens can be your best friends when raising and training a dog. Although they don't teach the dog not to chew the couch or pee on the carpet, they prevent inappropriate behaviors from becoming bad habits. Managing a dog's environment helps him to do the right things by limiting his choices. Preventing your dog from repeating negative patterns isn't the solution to all of your behavior problems, but it is integral.

For example, a fence is a management tool for dogs who enjoy playing in their yards and owners who want to keep them there. A baby gate in the kitchen limits the dog's freedom so that he can't get into trouble in the rest of the house while you're not around. And when you don't have time to teach your dog to sit for a guest, it's better to gate him off than allow him to dive on the visitor or bolt out the front door.

The Fallout of Punishment: Aggression

Punishment that is mistimed or too severe can often cause more serious problems. Dogs don't learn to like people or other dogs when they are corrected for barking and lunging. In fact, many of these animals become more unpredictable and aggressive, because they learn that the presence of other dogs or people means they are about to get punished.

Growling is a dog's way of warning us that he is uncomfortable and that there will be trouble if the bothersome person or dog doesn't go away. If you physically punish a dog for growling he might stop growling, but you could make him far more dangerous. Instead of warning people when he is distressed, he could just skip straight to the bite instead. You have, in essence, created a better biter. Punishing the warning doesn't make sense; we want to change the way the dog feels about the person or dog, not take away the warning that he is about to bite. Growling lets us know we have a problem and gives us time to do something about it—like teach the dog a positive association with people and dogs—before the dog bites.

Training versus Punishment

Never use punishment with any problem related to aggression around people or dogs—the risk of creating a better biter is just too high. Here are five reasons to teach your dog instead of punish him.

1. Punishment must be repeated frequently to remind the dog to avoid her mistake.
2. Punishment doesn't teach the dog anything; dogs with little confidence will wilt.
3. With punishment, you can't control what the dog learns.
4. Punishment can damage the relationship between owner and dog.
5. Punishment can accelerate aggression by suppressing all precursors to aggression, so the dog skips right to the bite.

There are many reasons not to use punishment, but in general, punishment misses the point and won't get you where you want to go. It comes too late to be instructive and has the danger of teaching the dog to be better at the very behavior you are trying to eliminate.

If you think you need to use punishment, it is probably an indicator of a much larger issue. Your dog needs more information about what she has to do to be right. Instead of spending your time figuring out how to stop the behaviors you don't like, map out what you do want your dog to do and retrain her.

The Kindness Revolution in Dog Training

It's clear that old methods of training—making the dog "obey"— are not only outdated, but also do not evolve your dog's problem-solving skills or intelligence. These days, it is easier to avoid using punishment because better alternatives are available.

It isn't necessary to use brute force or intimidation to make a dog comply; through use of a clicker, dog training has become kinder and gentler to both the dog and the owner. Clicker training isn't a gimmick or the latest fad; it is a scientifically based technique that uses the principles of operant conditioning. It's an intelligent, time-saving endeavor that promotes positive reinforcement through the use of treats and a clicker in order to teach your dog to think.

Training your dog with treats and a clicker is the fastest, most reliable way to teach your dog what you expect of him and have fun while you are doing it. There is no need to coerce, push, or shove to get what you want; once your dog knows how to learn, you will have a willing partner and a better overall relationship. Many families who have learned to train their dogs with a clicker and treats have enjoyed the learning process so much that they have come back again and again for more advanced classes.

The application of clicker training to dogs is pure genius; it simplifies and speeds up the process of learning for dogs and owners alike. Handlers of any age can learn the principles of clicker training, and since it is not dependent on corrections or physical manipulation, the size, strength, and stamina of the handler doesn't matter.

Using the Clicker

The clicker is a small plastic box with a metal tab that makes a clicking sound when you push down with your thumb. When the box is clicked the dog gets a treat, and after a few repetitions the dog learns to associate the sound of the clicker with a food reward. It's easy to find clickers at Petco and most other pet stores, or you can order them from dog training Web sites, such as *www.clickertraining.com*.

Why It Works

Pairing the clicker with a food reward is a powerful way to communicate to dogs about which behaviors are rewardable. Rather than helping your dog or physically manipulating his body, you teach your dog to learn by trial and error. Because the click noticeably marks the desired action, the dog is able to identify which behavior earned the reward (this is especially handy with a very active dog). When you click and then treat, the food reward is removed by a step. Eventually, you will find that your dog will work for the sound of the click rather than just a treat.

Think of the click as a snapshot of what the dog is doing at the exact moment he is doing it. This way, not only is it easier for the dog to understand what he is doing right, it also gets him excited about the learning process since it gives him the responsibility of making the click happen.

The Clicker as an Event Marker

Part of the reason why using a clicker is integral to successful training is because the sound of the click is unique and like nothing else the dog has heard. People often ask about using their voice instead of the clicker to mark appropriate behavior, but in the initial stages of training your voice is not a good event marker. Since you talk to your dog all the time, your voice does not have the same startling effect as the clicker. Because the clicker's unique sound reaches the part of the brain that is also responsible for the fight-or-flight response, it captures the dog's attention.

Shaping

Clicker training is all about the process of shaping behavior, which means breaking it down into steps that progress toward an end goal. Shaping is not a rigid list of steps, but rather a general guide to get from point A to point B with lots of room for variation, intuition, rapid progress (skipping steps), or reviewing if the steps are too big.

There are two types of shaping. Prompted shaping uses a food lure or target to elicit desired behaviors; free shaping requires you to wait for the dog to offer desired actions on his own, then reward him with a treat in order to capture the small steps that lead toward the end goal. With free shaping, the dog is fully in charge of which behaviors he is offering, so he will often learn faster (in some situations) and retain more than when you prompt his behavior with a lure or target. Keep in mind, however, that free shaping can be time consuming, since it depends upon the dog offering behavior, and this requires patience on the handler's part.

Whichever type of shaping you use, remember, you'll reach your goals faster if you have a plan, so keep notes on what you teach. Notice whether your dog catches on to the components as presented, or if she needs more explicit direction. Detailed notes make it easy to pick up where you left off, and your training sessions will be more productive overall.

Using Lures

A lure is a piece of food used to elicit behavior. Its goal is to help the dog get into the right position in order to earn the click and treat. It is often frustrating and time consuming for a beginning dog trainer to wait for the dog to offer the right behavior, so food lures often get things going. The problem with food lures is that unless they are faded relatively quickly, the dog (and humans) become dependent on them. If you continue to rely on food lures, you won't ever have a well-trained dog who obeys on cue; all you'll have is a dog who follows food.

Quick Fix: To Lure or Not to Lure?
For some dogs, lures are a great tool for prompting behavior. For others, however, lures present more of a distraction and hindrance than help. If this is true for your dog, you should skip lures altogether.

As a general rule, help the dog into position and lure her six times in a row. On the seventh repetition, do all the same motions with your body, but without the food lure in your hand. You can start fading the lure gradually by putting it on a nearby table and running to get it after the click. This way, the dog knows it's there and is excited about it but is not dependent on you waving it around to get her into the right position. Then, if the dog performs the behavior correctly, click and treat. If she doesn't perform the behavior correctly, go back and lure her six more times and try it again.

These mini drilling sessions train the dog to perform the correct behavior and show you if she understands what has prompted the click. This will help your dog to learn that she is working for the click, and that the treat is an afterthought.

Targeting

Targeting is a form of luring, but it removes the treat by a step by teaching the dog to touch his nose to an object. This tool can be used to move your dog or to have him interact with someone or something. Any item can be used, but the three main targets are your hand, a lid to a yogurt container, and a target stick. (You can buy a target stick online at *www.clickertraining.com* or make your own out of a short piece of dowel.) Keep in mind that the same rules apply regarding weaning dogs off of targets: Use targets to get the behavior started, and then slowly phase it out.

Hand Target

To teach your dog to target your hand with his nose, follow these steps:

1. Hold your hand palm-up with a piece of food tucked under your thumb in the center of your palm. Click and treat your dog for sniffing your hand.
2. Keep the food in your hand for six repetitions and then take the food out and repeat, clicking the dog for touching his nose to your palm.
3. Have the dog follow your hand in all directions while you move around the room.
4. Involve a helper and have your dog target your hand and then your helper's hand for clicks and treats.
5. Label the behavior of touching his nose to your hand by saying "Touch." (More on labeling follows.)
6. Try the trick in new places and with new people until your dog is fluent. Don't be afraid to go back to using food for a few repetitions if your dog falls apart around a new distraction.

Lid Target

On occasion, you might want your dog to move away from you to perform a behavior at a distance. In that case, it might be useful for you to teach your dog to target a yogurt lid with her nose. The steps for teaching your dog to target a lid are:

1. Put the lid in your hand and hold a treat in the center with your thumb.
2. When your dog noses at it, click and treat. Repeat six times.
3. Present the lid with no treat and click and treat for sniffing or nose bumping.

4. Label the behavior by saying "Touch" again just before your dog touches the lid.
5. Put the lid on the floor close by and repeat, clicking your dog at first for moving toward the lid and then for actually touching it with her nose.
6. Move the lid at varying distances until you can send her across the room to bump it with her nose for a click and treat.

Quick Fix: The Two-in-a-Row Rule
When training, try not to let your dog be wrong more than twice before helping him into the correct position, lessening the distraction, or changing the variables. If your dog makes more than two mistakes in a row, you need to change something so that he can be right more easily.

Stick Target

The target stick acts like an extension of your arm and is useful when working with your dog at a short distance. The steps for teaching your dog to touch a target stick with his nose are as follows:

1. Put the end of the stick in the palm of your hand with a treat and click and treat your dog for sniffing with his nose.
2. Gradually work your hand up the stick and only click and treat your dog for touching his nose close to the end away from your hand.
3. Try putting the stick on the floor and only clicking and treating when your dog touches the ends.
4. Have your dog follow the stick as you walk with him until he's racing to catch the end of it for a click and treat.

Paw Targeting

There are times when you might want your dog to use her paw to interact with an object. The difference between teaching your dog to target with her paw instead of her nose involves paying attention to which body part is hitting the target.

1. Put your hand or lid out for the dog to see, but withhold the click until she steps near it. Because you have already taught your dog to target with her nose, she might offer only this behavior at first. Be patient and wait for paw action near the target.
2. Withhold the click to let your dog know that you want something other than a nose touch and see what happens.
3. Make it easy on your dog by moving the lid or your hand along the floor so that you can click her for moving toward it. An easy way to help your dog to get this behavior started is to put the lid at the base of the stairs and click her for stepping on or next to it.
4. When you withhold the click your dog might get frustrated, but don't be too quick to help right away; wait and see if she'll paw at the target or move toward it.
5. Practice a paw target separately from a nose target and be sure to have two distinct cues for each one.
6. Keep in mind that short, frequent training sessions will help your dog figure out what you want faster than long, confusing ones.

For targeting to be useful, you must practice it often. The more experience your dog has with this method, the better it will serve you in your training.

Labeling Behavior

The major difference between clicker training and other types of training is that you don't label behaviors right away, because early versions are not what you want as the final result. A label can be a verbal cue, a hand signal, or both, but it should not be introduced until the dog offers a decent version of it. If you label behavior too soon you will get a wide variety of responses from the dog. But if you reserve the label until the behavior looks close to perfect, then you will be sure that the dog has properly connected what is being clicked.

 Quick Fix: On Cue
To replace an old cue with a new one, you need to present the new cue immediately before the old, exaggerated cue. Gradually make the exaggerated cue less exaggerated until the new cue prompts the behavior to occur.

You can call each behavior anything you want; just make it a simple one-syllable word as often as possible, and be sure it doesn't sound too much like any other word you use with your dog. Dogs pick up a lot from your body language and the pitch of your voice, but they sometimes have trouble distinguishing between similar sounding words, such as *no* and *go* for instance.

Weaning off the Clicker and Treats

Once your dog is reliably performing a behavior on cue (with 100 percent accuracy), he is ready to be weaned off the clicker and treats. (Remember: The click and treat always go together; don't click without treating because the value of the reward marker, the click, will become diluted and less meaningful to the dog.) The worst thing you can do when you are weaning your dog off the clicker and treats is to do it cold turkey, because it's too abrupt and frustrates the dog. Instead, wean gradually, by having your dog repeat a behavior more than once before you click and treat. This shows the dog that he must continue to perform the behavior until he hears his click.

The key to weaning is going slowly, getting the dog to perform longer versions of the behavior, or performing it in more repetitions successfully. The weaning process is a good time to start introducing nonfood rewards, such as the opportunity to greet a guest after sitting, or being released to play with other dogs after coming when called. However you do it, weaning your dog off extra commands and prompting accompanied by food lures will make you both relaxed in public, because you know what to expect from each other.

A Word on Food

Clicker training is successful because the emphasis is on the click, not the treat. Once dogs figure out the game, they love it and will gladly work regardless of how they feel about food. If you have a finicky fellow, try diversifying what you use as the reward and cutting back a little on his daily meal. For dogs who like to eat: Clicker training uses a lot of food rewards, but that doesn't mean you'll have a fat dog. Remember, the size of the rewards should be tiny— ¼ of an inch or less—and can even be drawn from the dog's meals. The length of your sessions should be five to ten minutes maximum, so your dog is not going to be getting a lot of extra treats at one time. If your dog is on a special diet, consult your veterinarian about what food treats you can use.

The beauty of clicker training is that it teaches dogs to think. It is a kind, nonviolent way to teach a dog what is expected of her. It is also long-lasting and easy, making it enjoyable for the trainer and trainee alike.

4: Solving Problems and Training Better Behaviors

By now you know that punishment is not the solution to your dog's problems, and you have an idea of some good alternatives for breaking inappropriate behaviors. Still, that recognition doesn't help a lot at times when your dog is driving you nuts with her incessant barking, whining, or nipping. You need only visit an animal shelter to see how many dogs between the age of nine months and two years have been left homeless, after their families simply gave up when they couldn't deal with their pup's antics. This sad situation is completely avoidable. Most families throw in the towel because they think their dog's behavior can't be fixed. In truth, they probably didn't put forth the time, energy, or dedication to socializing and training their dogs properly.

The root of many dogs' behavior problems lies in a lack of stimulation and energy outlets. Dogs are pack animals who are meant to live in groups; they are not solitary animals and do not enjoy spending hours alone for days at a time. Behavior problems don't have to lead to the dog being left at an animal shelter—you just need to understand how dogs think and what motivates them to do what they do.

When you take a dog into your home, you must make room for her. Dogs require a lot of love and training and care, but they give so much more back in loyalty and love. Be sure to give her the best home you possibly can—you will be rewarded a hundred fold. If your dog's behavior is less than ideal, don't give up on her. Remember that all dogs, no matter how sweet and compliant they are, need training, limits, exercise, and house rules.

The Power of Positive Reinforcement
For decades, animals in zoos, aquariums, and circuses have been trained using positive reinforcement. Can you imagine putting a training collar on a killer whale to try to make him jump? The same principle applies to dogs. Just because you can force dogs to obey doesn't mean you should. Don't force your dog to do anything—teach him to think instead!

Analyze the Problem

When it comes to solving their dog's behavior problems, people often think too much. For instance, they blame the dog for messing on the carpet out of spite when in reality the dog isn't being walked enough! Let's be clear here: Dogs don't hold grudges, and they don't do things out of spite. Dogs are not capable of those thoughts. They live in the moment, they are opportunistic, and they repeat behavior that is rewarded, even if it's rewarded negatively.

Dogs are animals, and animals do things that sometimes baffle humans, despite our best attempts to understand them. In order to solve an existing behavior problem, it is crucial to sit down with your family members and figure out the details of the problem. Using the following questions as a guide, try to identify and define what the dog is actually doing, when he is doing it, and what you might be able to teach him to do instead.

- **Identify the problem.** What does the dog actually do? Write it down and describe it in as much detail as possible.
- **Understand the cause.** What triggers the dog's behavior? Is it the presence of a strange dog, the doorbell, or a new person?
- **Think about frequency.** How often does the dog do the behavior? Only once in a while, or nonstop? Every time the trigger is present, or only half the time?
- **Consider the consequence.** What has been done to stop the behavior? What consequence results when the dog responds to the trigger?
- **Recognize reinforcement history.** How long has the dog been behaving this way, and what is reinforcing him to repeat the pattern?
- **Manage the problem.** What can you do to prevent the dog from continuing the behavior while you are retraining him?

By identifying the actual source of the problem, you will be able to develop a plan for retraining your dog to respond in a more appropriate way. Let everyone who takes care of the dog participate in the exercise, as well as in future training sessions.

Behavior Management

Prevention isn't training, but it can help you get rid of unwanted behavior, because you are not allowing the dog to practice it repeatedly. "Management" involves putting the dog in a separate room or crate when visitors arrive or stepping on the leash to prevent the dog from jumping. The less the dog gets to practice the wrong behavior, the less you will have to do to convince him that the right behavior is more rewarding and desirable. Behavior management does *not* mean correcting, reprimanding, or punishing your dog.

Some people manage their dog's behavior with crates, gates, and pens; others use leashes or time outs. It doesn't matter how you manage your dog's behavior, as long as it keeps your dog from practicing the wrong behavior over and over. Consider these behavior management ideas:

- Use a crate when you can't watch your dog if he is a destructive chewer.
- Keep a leash on your dog when company visits, and put your foot on it to prevent jumping.
- Don't allow your dog off leash in public places if he doesn't come when he's called.
- Avoid other dogs if your dog is aggressive around them.
- If your dog likes to escape out the front door, deny access to it.
- If your dog likes to bite the mailman, don't tie him outside the front door.
- If your dog is not fully housebroken, don't allow him unsupervised freedom.

Use management and prevention tactics to keep a behavior problem from perpetuating itself while you are retraining your dog to do something more appropriate. Prevention is not a 100-percent solution, but it can help you move toward your goal by not reinforcing inappropriate behavior.

Shape Up!
Free shaping is definitely worth adding to your bag of training tricks. It helps to give you lots of options in explaining what you want your dog to do. You just show up with your clicker and treats, then click and treat what you like and ignore what you don't.

Encouraging Alternate Behavior

Okay. You've gotten to the root of the bad behavior, and you have an interim plan in place—management. The next step is understanding reinforcement and replacement behavior. You need to provide reinforcement for a behavior other than the one you don't like. Otherwise, the dog will revert to the old behavior. Reinforce a behavior that is easy to teach and easy for the dog to perform, even with a lot of distractions.

Recognizing Negative Reinforcement

First off, look closely at the circumstances surrounding the misbehavior and see what your dog finds reinforcing about it. If he jumps and people yell at him and shove him off, perhaps he likes the attention and they should ignore him instead. Or maybe there is a member of your household who encourages the dog to jump and isn't consistent about reinforcing the dog for sitting instead.

Removing the source of the reinforcement will put a good dent in getting rid of a problem. In many cases the dog is getting too much response for the wrong behavior and needs more information about what is going right. If there isn't anything going right, then the dog has too much freedom and too many options. Then rethink your training program and make it easier for your dog to be right.

Reinforcing the Right Behavior

To change a behavior that has become habit, provide a high rate of reinforcement for the appropriate behavior or it won't occur to the dog to try anything else. Dogs do what works; if they get attention for the wrong behavior, they are likely to repeat it. But if they are reinforced for appropriate behavior with yummy treats or exciting games, they will make those good things happen again by repeating the behavior.

Every reinforcement for the right behavior is like money in the bank. If your dog's bank account for undesirable behavior is high, you will need to build up a considerable reinforcement history for the alternate behavior. Practice often, give occasional jackpots (a handful of small goodies or an extra-long game of fetch or tug), and set your dog up to succeed.

Training an Incompatible Behavior

Every time a dog practices an old, undesirable action, he builds up his bank account of negative behavior, so it's crucial to replace it with a more appropriate option. Make sure that the new behavior you teach instead is incompatible with the undesirable behavior. Teaching an acceptable replacement behavior solves many problems because a dog can't do two things at once. There's no way, for instance, for a dog to jump on a stranger if she's taught to sit politely when greeting a person. So if you reinforce sitting as the desirable behavior when your dog greets new people, eventually she won't even try to jump. Teaching your dog an alternate behavior gives you more control over her, and it also allows you to reward her for an appropriate response. Perhaps your dog could:

- Greet visitors with a toy in her mouth instead of jumping on them.
- Go to her bed or mat when the doorbell rings.
- Retrieve a toy instead of barking out the window at passersby.
- Look at you instead of lunging at other dogs.
- Target your hand (see Chapter 3) instead of running away.

Be forewarned: It takes lots of time and practice before a dog will learn to replace a negative behavior such as jumping with a more appropriate behavior like sitting and then offer it on her own.

Practice in short, frequent sessions, whenever opportunities present themselves. Don't forget that you can prevent negative activities from being an option—in the case of jumping, make sure you put your foot on the leash; this will enable your dog to be right more often.

Quick Fix: Don't Generalize
Dogs are not good at generalizing their behavior. They don't automatically transfer it to other surroundings. If you want to have control over your dog's behavior anywhere, train everywhere.

Once you pinpoint the causes and understand the triggers for your dog's inappropriate behavior, map out the changes you need to implement in your dog's routine, then determine a time frame for training him. Set up a schedule of consistent practice times to teach each part of each behavior in small, digestible portions you can build on. Be creative, make sure you provide for all of your dog's needs (mind and body), and find solutions that suit your dog's natural inclinations.

Self-control Exercise

It is integral to teach your dog self-control, because without it, she will never develop the concentration necessary for you to teach her basic obedience. The following example is a self-control exercise that helps your dog figure out how to pay attention to you. The Attention Game teaches your dog to check in with you often and to ignore distractions. In time, teaching your dog to check in with you will give him a greater awareness of you, which will improve his recall and heeling commands. (The Heel command teaches your dog to walk on your left side, regardless of your pace or direction, and to sit when you stop.) Dogs who have some responsibility to know where you are will not stray far away when they are off their leash. They will check in often and come back easily when you call because they know you are in control. Here's how the game works:

1. In a quiet room, sit in a chair with your dog on a leash.
2. Ignore your dog until she looks in your direction, then click and treat.
3. Ignore her again until she looks back at you, then click and treat.
4. Time yourself for one minute and count how many times she looks at you. If your dog looks at you six or more times in a minute, you are ready to add distractions.
5. Repeat this again in a new place or with a distraction and repeat the one-minute test. The distraction is too intense if your dog looks at you less than twice a minute.
6. Repeat this until your dog is looking at you six or more times a minute and then change the distraction again.
7. If your dog doesn't look at you more than twice in a minute for several repetitions, you will probably need to move away from the distraction or go somewhere less distracting.
8. Increase the quality and quantity of the rewards every once in a while to intensify the dog's response and to increase the likelihood that she will look at you more often.
9. Jackpot exceptional behavior. If your dog ignores an unexpected distraction, be sure to reward her with a whole handful of goodies to reinforce the good performance.

Your goal with this game is to focus your dog's attention on you. When your dog pays attention to you, he's learning to block out distractions and maintain self-control. Once he can do this successfully, you're ready to move on to more specific commands.

Teaching Basic Commands

Nothing beats the companionship of a well-trained dog. A dog who responds to Sit, Down, and Come is a dog who can be taken many places without putting you to shame. These commands go a long way in helping you to replace unwanted behaviors. The better your dog responds to these common commands, the easier it will be to teach more complicated ones. Spend time teaching these basics, at first in an environment with few distractions, then build up to working outdoors or around other dogs or people.

Sit

Teaching Sit involves luring the dog into position before you click and treat for the correct response. Remember that when using a lure, it's important to fade its presence quickly to keep the dog from becoming dependent upon it (see Chapter 3). Fading a lure is an important part of making sure your dog becomes reliable and is truly grasping the concept of sitting. The steps to teaching Sit are as follows:

► **Miniature Pinscher being lured to sit**

1. Hold a treat slightly above your dog's nose and bring it back slowly over his head.
2. When your dog's bottom hits the ground, click and treat.
3. If your dog keeps backing up, practice against a wall so he can only go so far.
4. Repeat this until your dog is offering Sit readily.
5. Take the treat out of your hand and, holding your hand the same way, entice your dog to Sit. If he Sits, click and treat; if he doesn't, go back to using a food lure for six to eight more repetitions.
6. Once your dog is doing this reliably, verbally label the behavior "Sit" right before the dog's bottom hits the ground.
7. Repeat these steps in various places until your dog is responding well with no mistakes.
8. Now, without a treat in your hand, ask your dog to repeat the behavior more than once before you click and treat. Start with low numbers of repetitions like two, three, or four Sits before you click and treat, but don't follow a pattern.
9. To help him generalize the behavior, practice in new places—the pet store, the park, the vet's office. Remember that forgetting is a normal part of learning and you will need to go back to helping the dog, with a treat in your hand if necessary, if the place you are working in is very distracting.
10. To test your dog's training, try for ten in a row. If he gets less than 100 percent, go back to practicing before asking for the behavior in that environment.

If your dog fails the Ten in a Row rule, you need to help him for a few repetitions before he attempts the exercise again without help. Going back to the previous steps to help your dog get into the right position gives him information about what he needs to do to earn his click and treat and prevents him from getting confused and frustrated.

Sitting Pretty

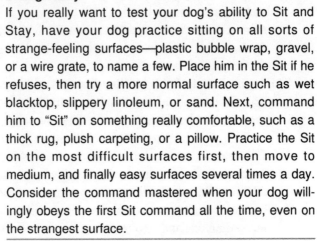

If you really want to test your dog's ability to Sit and Stay, have your dog practice sitting on all sorts of strange-feeling surfaces—plastic bubble wrap, gravel, or a wire grate, to name a few. Place him in the Sit if he refuses, then try a more normal surface such as wet blacktop, slippery linoleum, or sand. Next, command him to "Sit" on something really comfortable, such as a thick rug, plush carpeting, or a pillow. Practice the Sit on the most difficult surfaces first, then move to medium, and finally easy surfaces several times a day. Consider the command mastered when your dog willingly obeys the first Sit command all the time, even on the strangest surface.

Sit/Stay

Turning the Sit into a Sit/Stay involves two processes: getting the dog to hold the position for longer periods of time (duration), and holding the position while the handler moves further away (distance). If you teach this behavior in two steps you will have a reliable dog who doesn't fall apart around distractions. The steps for teaching duration include the following:

1. Get your dog into a Sit and then count to two before you click and treat.
2. Gradually increase the time the dog has to hold the behavior by several seconds before you click and treat, until you can build it up to ten seconds between each click and treat.
3. When you can get to ten seconds, verbally label it "Stay" and give the hand signal (most people use a flat, open palm toward the dog).
4. Increase the time between each click and treat randomly to

keep the dog guessing as to how long she must wait for her next click.

5. Add in distractions, and start from the first step to rebuild the behavior of Sit/Stay around new variables.

The second part of the Sit/Stay command involves the dog holding the Sit while you move away from her. The steps for teaching your dog to hold her position relative to yours are:

1. Get your dog into a Sit and take a small step right or left, returning immediately. If your dog maintains her position, click and treat. If she doesn't, do a smaller movement.

2. Gradually shift your weight, leaving your hands in front of the dog. Click and treat the dog for maintaining her position in front of you. Practice this gradual movement until the dog is convinced she should stay in one spot.

3. Increase the distance slowly and keep moving at first, never staying in one spot too long without coming back to the dog to click and treat. Standing still too soon in the process will cause your dog to run to you.

4. Once you are able to cross the room with your dog maintaining her position, start to stay away a few seconds longer before coming back.

5. Increase the time slowly so that you are combining both the length of time the dog holds the position (duration) and how close or far you are from the dog (distance).

Down/Stay

When teaching your dog to Lie Down and Stay for extended periods, pay attention to the surface you are asking him to lie on. Make sure it isn't extreme in temperature, and that it isn't so hard and uncomfortable that your dog fidgets. Short-coated dogs are often uncomfortable on hardwood or linoleum floors, and will learn to lie down more readily on a carpet or towel.

1. Starting with your dog in the Sit position, use a treat to lure his nose about halfway to the floor. When your dog follows the treat by lowering his head, click and treat.
2. Gradually lower your hand closer to the floor. You might need to go back to a food lure for a few reps if your dog seems stuck and won't lower his head any further.
3. When you get the treat to the floor, experiment with holding it out under your hand, or closer to and under his chest, and wait. Most dogs will fool around for a while trying to get the treat and then plop to the ground. When your dog goes all the way down, click and treat.
4. Repeat this six times with a treat, clicking and treating each time your dog goes all the way down.
5. Now, without a treat in your hand, make the same hand motion and click and treat for any attempt to lie down.
6. If your dog fails more than twice, go back to using a treat for six more times and then try again.
7. Take it on the road. When you go somewhere new or involve distractions like other dogs and people, the behavior might fall apart a bit. Don't be afraid to go back to using a food lure to show the dog what to do and then fade it out when the dog is performing the behavior reliably.

Some dogs have trouble lying down and seem to get stuck in the sitting position. Here are some tips for dogs who get stuck.

- Practice on a soft surface away from distractions at first.
- Use novel treats that the dog loves but hardly ever gets.

- Use a low table, the rung of a chair, or even your out-stretched leg to lure the dog low to the ground and under the object to give her the idea.
- Experiment with holding the treat closer to the dog's body and between the front paws close to the chest, or further away from her nose at a 45-degree angle.
- Avoid pushing to get her down. As soon as you start pushing, the dog turns her brain off and stops thinking about what she's doing, letting you do the work. If you want to teach your dog to think, don't push or pull her into position.

Verbalize Effectively

When verbally labeling commands, it's important to use the right tonality, inflection, and volume. Never plead, mumble, or shout. Always preface verbal commands with the dog's name. The name and command should sound like one word: "Buster come," rather than "Buster . . . come." This way, it will be clear to your dog that you are speaking to him, and there won't be any hesitation. Just one exception: Don't use your dog's name in conjunction with the "Stay" command. Since hearing his name implies he should be attentive and ready to go, you would be sending a mixed message. Whenever you use a verbal command, remember only to say it once!

Come

Teaching your dog to Come when you call him has more to do with the status of your relationship than anything else you've done to this point. If your dog believes that you are in charge, he knows that you control everything good and that he must check in with you often in order to have access to the things he wants. Review the section on leadership earlier in this book and try to be diligent about becoming a strong and fair leader.

The first thing a dog must do to Come is turn away from what she wants and look back in your direction. To teach a strong foundation for Come, follow these steps:

1. Start with the dog on her leash in a slightly distracting area, keep her from the things she wants, and wait for her to look back at you, then click and treat.
2. Repeat this until the dog no longer looks away from you.
3. Change the distraction, go somewhere more stimulating, or go closer to the distractions and repeat.
4. If your dog doesn't look back at you in thirty seconds or less, move further away from the distraction until she will look at you within that time.
5. When your dog is looking back at you predictably, run backward as you click and deliver the treat at your feet to encourage the dog to catch you.
6. As your dog gets good at this, wait until she is on her way back to you before you click.
7. Verbally label this behavior "Come" as your dog gets to you to eat her treat.
8. Change the distractions. Increase the intensity of a distraction by going closer to it or increasing the distance between you and your dog by using a longer leash.
9. If your dog doesn't respond by looking back in a reasonable amount of time, back away from the distraction.

The trick to teaching Come is to set your dog up to be successful. Don't allow off-leash freedom if your dog is not reliable, and practice, practice, practice! After establishing a firm foundation for Come on a six-foot leash, then use a longer leash, and go back and review all of the steps from the beginning. Some dogs will make great progress quickly, and others will need you to go much slower so that they can be successful.

Gradually increase the length of the leash until your dog can turn away from what he wants (the foundation for coming when called) and come back to you easily, then progress to dropping the leash and letting him drag it, and eventually take it off while reviewing all the steps to teach Come. When you first take off the leash, you might want to practice in a fenced or protected area in case you've hurried your dog's training and he runs off and won't respond. This just means that you need to back up a few steps and put the leash back on for a while.

Quick Fix: Keep Your Hands to Yourself

Some dogs, although they learn to respond to the Come command, will stay just out of reach or dart right past you. Without realizing it, owners sometimes encourage their dogs to cut their approach and stay farther away by attempting to cradle, caress, or hug the dog. Petting your dog as he arrives can create or worsen recall problems because extending your arms makes it appear as if you are protecting the space in front of you. Instead of reaching for your dog, use verbal praise to acknowledge, encourage, and congratulate your dog's arrival.

Though the process seems a bit long and tedious, it is well worth the effort, because you will have a dog who comes to you reliably when you call her. As your dog gets good at checking in with you, you can begin to offer real-life rewards mixed in with treats, like the freedom to go back to playing with another dog, the opportunity to sniff a spot on the ground, or the chance to chase a squirrel. If these opportunities are given as rewards your dog will learn that coming to you and checking in on a regular basis is a good thing. Regardless of how well your dog learns to come when called however, remember never to allow him off leash in unsafe areas where a mistake could cost him his life.

Make a Plan and Chart Your Dog's Progress

As you shape your training plan, break down each behavior you teach into individual steps and track your dog's progress—and stumbling blocks. Get in the habit of examining your dog's success rate and periodically re-evaluate your shaping plan, making adjustments as necessary. Use the Ten in a Row rule as a general guide. Once your dog can repeat a step with 100 percent accuracy, you are ready to progress to the next step. If your dog makes a lots of mistakes or acts disinterested, break things down into smaller steps or change your approach in some way.

Periodically review the behavioral questions explained earlier in this chapter with your family, and think about how you want your dog to respond in different situations. Remember to use your training log—it's an important part of a successful program, because your notes provide a bit of history on your progress. If you run into a snag along the way, you can review the steps where you were most successful, see what worked, and make changes so you can keep moving forward.

Most importantly, stop reinforcing incorrect behavior and start reinforcing a better alternative behavior in its place. When choosing which behaviors to reinforce, remember the following things.

Keep It Simple

Whatever you choose as the alternate behavior, it should be simple for the dog to offer quickly and reliably. Choose a single behavior, like Sit or Down, and reinforce it often. If the behavior is too complicated or involved, your dog might lose interest and revert to the undesirable behavior. A simple behavior like Sit is something you are likely to notice and reinforce even in a distracting environment. Be sure your dog knows the behavior well by applying the Ten in a Row rule.

Plan Ahead for Success

If you want to ensure your dog responds to your commands everywhere, you have to train him everywhere. Learning in a variety of environments is more like real life for the dog, and the learning tends to become more permanent because the dog begins to realize that her commands work everywhere. Dogs pick things up quickly, but they're lousy generalizers. They tend to revert back to old, ingrained behaviors in new environments, so if you haven't taught your dog to sit when greeting strangers at the park, for example, he won't try that off the bat. The more distractions a dog gets to practice around, the quicker she will learn to generalize her response to your commands in all sorts of environments.

Always anticipate instances where you'll be able to reinforce the right behavior and prevent the wrong one. Keep a leash hanging by the door so that you are ready to thwart jumping on guests, and have a container of treats ready to reinforce sitting. Also carry your clicker and treats with you at all times. It might seem awkward at first, but it is essential for capturing and reinforcing your dog's behavior at the exact moment she makes the right choice. If you're ever not prepared to click and treat, then shower your pup with lots of praise and pats, or games and other opportunities to acknowledge her good behavior.

Control the Variables

Distractions often ruin the best-laid training plans simply because they are too stimulating for a dog to ignore. Controlling the variables means controlling what's shifting your dog's attention away from you. Common variables include things that move, such as balls, off-leash dogs, cars, kids, and runners; environmental factors, like being outside; or the presence of food.

If you want your dog to succeed around distractions, it's essential to control the distance between your dog and the distraction, as well as manage the frequency, type, and intensity of the distraction. If you handle these things properly, you will increase the speed with which your dog learns. If ringing the doorbell sends your dog into a frenzy, for example, you might first want to work on desensitizing him to the doorbell sound; then you can move on to greeting the visitor. In this case, the dog's response to the doorbell and the dog's response to the person should be considered two separate issues.

You will immediately notice how important the distance between your dog and the action is during your training sessions, so find your dog's critical distance, and work from there. The distance at which he notices the distraction but will still perform the behavior is the starting point. Then, in subsequent training sessions, decrease that distance until he is able to work while the distractions are close to him.

Pay close attention to the level of distraction you are working with. To decrease the intensity of a distraction, offer less movement, fewer dogs, people, or other visual stimuli before attempting to teach the dog anything. As your dog learns to ignore distractions and perform the behavior well, you can gradually increase the intensity until he is working in the middle of the distraction.

Over time, train your dog to pay attention and respond regardless of what else is going on. Doing this in slow progressions will help you attain your goals quickly and reliably.

Breed-Specific Behavior Problems

Dogs with persistent problems are often exhibiting behavior related to the job they were bred to do. When a dog has a problem related to his original working ability, think of it as genetically hard-wired. Consider the Border Collie who chases and nips at heels, or the Retriever obsessed with having everything in her mouth.

To change your dog's mind about a behavior that is this instinctive, provide extra reinforcement for the behavior you are trying to teach instead. Keep your standards low at first, and reward the dog for even attempting the new behavior. Don't up your criteria or expect multiple repetitions; simply reward the new behavior as often as possible. Building a strong reinforcement history takes time and practice, but it can eventually replace old hard-wired behaviors with new, desirable ones.

Set for Success

It's human nature to notice what is going wrong and point it out. But pointing out mistakes only acts as reinforcement, and it can actually teach a person or animal to make the same mistake over and over again. All you can do is make a difference in a future behavior by setting the animal up for success. Limit her options, prevent the wrong behaviors, provide good consequences for the correct choices, and follow through with consequences for the wrong ones. When an animal has choices, learning is more permanent and consequences will directly shape her response.

Behavior problems need not be a mystery. You *can* figure out why your dog behaves in certain ways and then devise solutions to teach your dog concentration, self-control, and obedience in order to redirect the behavior. By doing so, you won't become just another one of the many frustrated dog owners who give up.

5: Housebreaking 101

Housebreaking problems are the leading cause of people giving up their animals to shelters across the nation. Nothing erodes the bond between human and dog quicker than a puddle or a pile on the carpet. No need to fret, though. Dogs have a natural inclination toward housebreaking: By instinct, they will not eliminate in the same area where they sleep. We can take advantage of this tendency to help us train them quickly and successfully.

When Nature Doesn't Run Its Course

Despite this natural inclination, there are several reasons why a new dog might have difficulties with housebreaking. In some cases, the puppy was not raised by a super-clean mom who kept the whelping box free of stool. In others, the puppy might have spent too much time in a cage at a pet store or a shelter and learned to go in her crate because there was no other option. Either way, a puppy who doesn't have this instinct can be more difficult to housebreak. This doesn't mean they can't learn to go in the appropriate place; the process will just take a little longer and require you to be more vigilant and flexible with your walking schedule.

Proper housebreaking should be the first order of business for anyone who brings home a new puppy, yet almost all house-breaking problems are caused by human error. Often, humans don't set proper limits or allow too much freedom too soon. Some pups have free run of the house before they are housebroken, so they go to the bathroom whenever they have to go, and they never learn to hold it. Other pups are not supervised well enough when they do have freedom and sneak off to "go" somewhere inappropriate when no one is looking. The good news is that all you need to do is educate yourself, and then you, too, can have a pooch who knows where to eliminate.

Using a Crate to Housebreak Your Dog

The dog's ancestor, the wolf, housebroke himself by sleeping in a cave and eliminating outside. Through adults' examples, puppies learned to do the same. We mimic this cave concept when we crate train our dogs. Using a crate is like giving your dog his own bedroom, a place for him to relax and rest without getting into trouble. Crates are not just for housebreaking—they also keep your puppy safe while you are away and prevent destructive behavior.

Young puppies, or even adult dogs, who are not housebroken should not have free access to the house. Too much freedom too soon creates housebreaking problems. Dogs often consider where they eat and sleep their home and treat the rest of the house as if it were outside. That is why a puppy kept in the kitchen will often run to the dining room and piddle or poop if he gets loose. Keeping your puppy confined in his crate when you cannot watch him is an excellent housebreaking tool, because it requires that he hold his bladder and bowels to avoid an unpleasant consequence (having to sit in his own mess until you come to rescue him).

Using a crate gives a clear message to a puppy: "Hold it until I let you out." Using a crate is not mean; it's the nicest thing you can do for your dog, and if it's used properly it will help speed up housebreaking. Following are some tips for using a crate:

1. A young puppy (less than sixteen weeks) should be in the crate more than she is out; she should only be free when you are there to supervise her.
2. No food or water should be given in the crate while you are gone.
3. No cozy blankets, towels, or padding should be used in the crate until he's been dry in there for at least two weeks straight. Otherwise, he might go on the towel and then kick it to the back.
4. A puppy between the ages of eight and twelve weeks will need to be taken to the potty spot, to see if she needs to go, every hour at first and then every two to three hours after that.
5. Hire a pet sitter to provide regular walks if you are gone for long periods during the day.
6. Puppies twelve to eighteen weeks can last a bit longer between walks, but you should increase the time gradually.
7. If your pup cries or barks in the crate, try to ignore him until he is quiet before letting him out. Covering the crate completely with a sheet or towel often helps puppies settle down to sleep faster, especially if they bark and whine a lot.
8. Use the clicker and treats to shape your puppy going in and out of the crate.
9. Put your puppy in the crate frequently when you are home so that she gets used to being away from you for gradually longer periods of time.
10. Keep your crate around throughout the first and second year of your dog's life. You will find it a godsend if you have workmen doing repairs, company visiting, or if you travel

with your dog. If you teach your dog to like his crate, he will always have a safe place to call his own.

An extra word of warning: Often, young puppies will cry, whine, bark, or howl *incessantly* when they want to get out of the crate—especially at night. As tempting as it might be to let her out when you are desperate to go back to sleep, unless your puppy is trying to tell you she has to go to the bathroom, don't give in. She'll never learn if you're not consistent.

For dogs who cannot be crate trained for some reason, using baby gates as a means of confinement is key. Keep the confinement area relatively small, so your puppy does not designate one end of the space for sleeping, and the other for going to the bathroom. If the dog is walked on a regular basis, however, he will do his best to keep his gated area clean.

In any case, whenever an unhousebroken dog is not crated he should be supervised constantly. A dog should not be allowed to have free access to the house until he has been reliable with his housebreaking for at least six weeks. Freedom after that should be given gradually until you are certain your dog is housebroken.

Choosing the Right Crate

Crating is widely accepted by behaviorists, dog trainers, veterinarians, and knowledgeable dog owners as a humane means of confinement. It not only deters soiling, it prevents stealing, shredding, chewing, scratching, or any other type of unwanted mischief your dog might get into while you're not around. You should feel as comfortable about crating your pup in your absence as you would about securing a toddler in a highchair at mealtime. Just be sure to keep the following points in mind when choosing a crate:

- **Size:** A crate should be large enough for the dog to stand without his shoulders touching its ceiling, but not so big that there is enough space for him to soil on one end and then lie away from the mess at the other end.
- **Safety:** Homemade enclosures might save you money, but how would you feel if your pup pokes himself in the eye, swallows wood splinters, wallpaper, or bits of blankets, or gets caught on his crate because you ignored potential dangers? Make sure there are no protrusions, sharp edges, or components he might accidentally ingest.
- **Proximity:** Keep your dog's crate in an area where he feels safe and comfortable. If your dog is prone to chewing, scratching, or jumping up, make sure you position his crate far enough away from any woodwork, linoleum, furniture, counters, garbage, or windows he might be able to get at while he's in there.

▶ **Miniature Pinscher stepping out of her crate**

Tracking Your Dog's Schedule

Teaching a dog to use the outside for her bathroom needs is not rocket science, but it can be frustrating and time consuming. Housebreaking tricks won't teach your dog to go outside overnight, but they will make sure you are moving in the right direction. One useful tool is keeping a chart on the fridge that marks what time your dog was walked, if she went, and what she did. This will help the whole family keep track of your puppy's progress, which will make it easier to know when your puppy should be supervised carefully for signs that she has to go out (most puppies will sniff the floor and walk in circles). The chart will also help you to know when your pup is ready for some freedom.

Housebreaking Habits

A young pup between seven and twelve weeks should be walked every hour. Being taken to the same spot time and again gives him the idea of what he needs to do and where to do it. Pick one spot in the yard, keep him on a leash, and only stay out for about one to three minutes. (If you allow a puppy to roam the yard on his own, chances are he'll have so much fun he'll forget to go, then come inside and have an accident on the floor.) If he goes when you take him outside, label it and play with him, or give him a little freedom in the house or yard. If he doesn't go he should be crated or kept with you; try again in ten or twenty minutes.

As your puppy gets to be between twelve and sixteen weeks old, you'll find that he can go longer between potty trips. Use your chart to decide how long that should be. Your chart will also help you to keep track of when your puppy has accidents so that you will know when you need to add in an extra walk or supervise more carefully. After several weeks of charting, you will be able to determine if you are making progress in the right direction, and if you aren't, what you need to do to get back on track.

No Papers, Please

If you want to housebreak your dog reliably, don't use newspaper or potty pads. It's the surest way to make her unreliable with housebreaking. Dogs who are trained to "go" on newspaper or potty pads never learn to hold it because they go whenever they have to. Take her outside from day one and don't look back. If you are currently using newspaper, throw it away right now!

Using a Leash for Potty Trips

Unless your dog is a rescue dog adopted from a shelter as an adult and absolutely will not go on a leash, it is a good idea to use a leash to take your dog to the potty spot. The leash allows you to communicate to your dog that you are not outside to play but to take care of the business at hand. The leash should be about six feet long and you should stand in one spot; don't follow the dog all over the yard. Let the dog sniff in a circle around you and praise the heck out of him if he goes. Try not to get him into the habit of walking the neighborhood unless you want to do that in freezing cold weather or pouring rain. Walking your dog on a leash will teach him to go to the bathroom quickly and on demand, without too much distraction.

Label It

Dogs who are taught to go to the bathroom on cue are a pleasure to walk. Even in bad weather they go out and do their business, and their owners don't freeze to death waiting for them. Labeling the act of eliminating will put it on cue and help you to speed up the process. Common labels for potty behavior are Go, Hurry Up, or Get Busy.

Label potty behavior by saying your command as your dog is in the process of going. You can even click and treat as she is going to give her the idea that doing her business outside is a good thing. It takes a lot of repetitions for the dog to understand that the command means to "Go," so be patient and make sure everyone in the family knows which commands are being used.

Quick Fix: Background Noise
No matter how badly you feel about leaving your dog home alone in the crate, never leave the TV or radio on as company, because he might find the programming too unsettling or noisy. It's better to replace that cacophony with some sort of white noise, such as the whir of a fan.

Training your dog to go on command is really convenient—just think how much easier it then is to take him inside a store, to a friend's house, or even to the hospital if you want to visit as a therapy dog team. If you know your dog has gone and will last until you leave, you can relax and enjoy your visit.

Making a Potty Spot in Your Yard

You might want to consider creating a designated potty spot where your dog can do his business without interfering with the rest of your yard. Creating one area that clearly says "bathroom" to your dog will not only help you housebreak him, it will also keep him from using the whole yard as his toilet. This comes in handy when you want to have barbecues or your children want to play outside, because you won't have to worry about scooping the whole yard.

To build the potty spot, you'll want to use materials that offer good drainage and the ability to disinfect. Here are some potty spot recommendations:

- Make a square or rectangular box out of garden timbers cut to the dimensions you wish. Large dogs probably need an 8-foot x 8-foot area, whereas smaller dogs could probably get by with a 4-foot x 4-foot space.
- Cover the bottom with several bags of sand.
- Cover the sand with a variety of sizes of crushed stone. Some people prefer the tiny size often called "pea stone"; others prefer the 1-inch diameter.

Designated potty spots will allow you to scoop easily and disinfect with a bleach solution regularly. A weed sprayer with a 30:70 solution of bleach and water works well as a disinfectant. Even in tight quarters, this arrangement eliminates excessive odors and unsanitary conditions. A metal rake will also come in handy for redistributing the stone and sand.

Controlling Food and Water

A puppy is like a sieve: What goes in will come out. Pay attention to how much and how often she eats and drinks; if you regulate what goes in, you can also regulate what comes out. Your unhousebroken dog should not have free access to food and water, because she will eat and drink whenever she wants, and you will be less able to predict when she'll need to go out. In order to housebreak a dog, you need to stick to a strict food and water schedule and be sure that she is walked at regular intervals. Puppies that have a regular feeding routine are easy to predict; if you feed and water them on a schedule, they will go out on schedule.

The best way to help a puppy develop a reliable housebreaking schedule is to feed roughly at the same time each day and not leave water out all day and night. Put the food down for ten minutes; then pick it up if he doesn't finish and put it away until the next meal. Feed a young pup seven to twelve weeks old three times a day; an older puppy or adult dog can eat twice a day.

Puppies should have plenty of fresh, clean water, except while crated or about two hours before bedtime. Give water at regular intervals—at least five times a day—and then be ready to take him out when necessary. Just before bedtime, take your puppy outside, and then no more water for the rest of the night once you crate him. (Remember: Very young puppies might have to be taken out once during the night.)

With pups who urinate frequently, you might try restricting water. But before you do, tell your veterinarian about your plans. He or she might want to perform some diagnostic tests beforehand to rule out bladder or urinary tract problems. In severe cases where, despite a clean bill of health, the pup still continually urinates, offer water only before taking him out to relieve himself. With pups who just can't seem to hold it throughout the night, withhold water for three hours before going to bed.

Don't Punish Mistakes

If your puppy has an accident, it's probably not her fault because, most likely, you forgot to walk her at the right time. If you'd like to hit yourself over the head with a rolled up newspaper, feel free, but don't punish your puppy. Your puppy won't learn not to go in the house by being scolded. What she will learn is to avoid going in front of you and instead go under the dining-room table when no one is looking. The end result is that it will be nearly impossible to get her to go on a leash, because she will come to believe that going in front of someone is wrong.

It is a much better strategy, therefore, simply to reward your dog when he is successful. When he makes mistakes, just ignore him for a while. Put him in a crate or gated room, clean up the mess, and make a note of the time of the accident. Keep track of your dog's mistakes to see if there is a pattern to them, so you know if you should add in extra walks.

Creating a Good Crate Environment

If you only use the crate to shut your dog in when it's time to leave him, he might develop a bad association with crating. Instead, practice with him frequently and teach him to go into the space on his own, without always closing the door behind him, so that he feels happy and safe there. Although you should never feed a dog his meals in a crate, you might want to sprinkle a few pieces of kibble or some yummy bites of cold cuts or cheese on the bottom of the crate when you are around, to entice him. Then, when he runs in and gobbles the snack up, you can praise him, and it will help him become accustomed to going in and out of his crate.

Cleaning Up Accidents

When your puppy has an accident on the carpet or floor, it is essential to clean it up as quickly and as thoroughly as possible to eliminate lingering odors, because any remaining smell will draw the puppy back to that spot. Here are some tips for cleaning up urine on carpet:

1. Blot up as much as possible with paper towels.
2. Pour an eight-ounce glass of water over the spot to dilute the urine.
3. Blot until there is no hint of yellow left on the paper towels.
4. Spray carpet cleaner over the entire spot and scrub with a brush or a sponge.
5. Spray the area again and follow the product's directions for standing time and vacuuming. (Repeat as needed.)
6. Spray with an enzyme inhibitor, which eliminates the odor, following product directions exactly.

Quick Fix: Umbilical Cording

A crate-trained dog is not necessarily house-trained. Your dog still needs supervised exploration to learn the house rules. When your dog is out of his crate, keep your eyes glued on him or, better still, umbilical cord him so he'll follow you. This will cut misbehaviors short before they become habits.

Tie his leash to your belt on your left side. Give him only enough slack to keep him at your side without your legs becoming entangled. If he attempts to jump, chew, bark, or relieve himself, you'll be able to stop him instantly by tugging the lead. This way, you can train your dog while you work or relax at home.

Cleaning up feces on carpet can be tricky. Remove as much as possible with paper towels before treating the area to avoid rubbing the excess into the carpet and thereby compounding the problem.

1. Remove all solid waste with paper towels.
2. Spray with carpet cleaner and rub out as much as possible with a sponge.

3. Spray the area again and use a scrub brush to deep clean the fibers of the carpet.
4. Spray the area with carpet cleaner again and follow the product's directions for standing time and vacuuming. (Repeat as needed.)
5. Spray with enzyme inhibitor (available in most pet stores) to eliminate the odor permanently.
6. Consider rearranging the furniture to block access to that spot if your dog continues to go back to it over and over.

Cleaning up urine or feces on hardwood floors should be done a little differently to prevent permanent damage to the floor.

1. Wipe up excess with paper towels.
2. Mix up a bucket of Murphy's Oil Soap and water and wash the area thoroughly with a mop or sponge.
3. Dry the area thoroughly with a rag or paper towels.
4. Spray an enzyme inhibitor (made especially for this purpose) on a cloth and wipe down the area one last time.

Cleaning any area where an accident occurred is essential to keeping your dog on track with his housebreaking. If you are cleaning up more than a couple of accidents a week, you are probably not walking your puppy outside often enough or are allowing too much freedom too soon. Remember that limiting a puppy's freedom is half the key to housebreaking, and it's only temporary until your puppy proves he knows where to "go" and is completely reliable.

Dogs need to go out at least once during a four-hour period if confined to a small area, like a crate. If they have more freedom or free access to food and water, they might have to go more frequently. Most adult housebroken dogs need to be walked first thing in the morning, sometime midday, after work, and before bed. A midday visit from a pet sitter can help your adult dog maintain his excellent housebreaking manners.

Quick Fix: Do Some Detective Work

If you are not sure you know about all the spots where your dog has messed in the house, consider purchasing a black light (available in some dog supply catalogs) to detect urine stains on the carpet.

Occasionally a dog might have a medical problem that is interfering with housebreaking. If you were making good progress with housebreaking but your dog suddenly regresses, consider having your veterinarian check a urine and stool sample for signs of infection or parasites. These conditions often present themselves as a regression in a housebreaking program, but they can be easily treated with medication.

If, despite your best efforts, you find your dog's housebreaking problems still baffle you, or if you adopted an older dog who came with a host of serious behavioral problems, you might want to consider the help of a professional dog trainer or behaviorist.

It's silly to give up a dog who lacks good housebreaking back to the shelter or pound, but living with a dog who uses your house as her bathroom is no picnic either. Housebreaking is the most basic training issue that must be accomplished if a dog is going to live well with humans. Remember, the tricks to housebreaking come down to some very basic elements: Confine your dog in some way, put her on a schedule, keep track of her successes and failures, control her food and water bowls, walk her outdoors in short, frequent spurts, and avoid punishing her mistakes. If you follow these guidelines your dog should be making fairly good progress within a month to six weeks' time.

6: The Bark Stops Here

What is more maddening than listening to nonstop barking from a dog whose careless owner tied her up outside and then left for hours? Dogs bark to communicate with us and with each other, but excessive barking is inappropriate and a symptom of a larger problem. If a dog barks too much, it means that the dog's mental, emotional, and physical needs are not being met. This problem must be addressed first, if peace and quiet are to reign.

Why Do Dogs Bark Excessively?

Barking is a common problem for dog owners—and it's often the top complaint of neighbors stuck listening to the restless protests of a bored dog. Dogs are pack animals with strong bonds to their family members; it is unnatural for them to be alone for hours at a time. In their boredom and frustration they tend to bark, which is self-reinforcing. Barking is an emotional release, a way for a dog to express her emotion and let out bottled-up anxiety and dissatisfaction.

A dog who barks too much falls into one of three categories: the dog who barks when left alone; the dog who barks at visitors, noise, and people passing by while you are home; and the dog who barks at you for attention. Whichever is the case, it generally means that the dog is either lacking something she needs, or she is being consistently reinforced for the wrong behavior.

Meeting Your Dog's Needs

All dogs need a healthy diet, a predictable schedule, lots of exercise, interaction with people and other dogs, training, a safe place to sleep and rest, and a stimulating environment with toys and things to chew. Dogs also need to be taught from the time they are puppies to be content when they are away from you, so that they come to expect that you will return predictably to take care of them.

Dogs who are with their owners all the time (perhaps you work from home or are a stay-at-home parent) can also become excessive barkers when their owners do leave them even briefly. These dogs become inappropriately bonded to their owners, and in their absence find it difficult to cope. Such overattachment between owners and dogs can erode the dogs' self-confidence and contentment when they are alone. Take a moment to examine how much or how little time you spend with your dog and make the necessary adjustments to help her feel confident and secure.

Mindful Management

The next few sections review some basic elements of what you need to keep in mind while you come up with a plan to curb (or at least cut down) your dog's barking. The philosophy is the same for training any behavior: Have a plan, be patient, be consistent, and reinforce the right behaviors.

Doin' What Comes Naturally

Some types of dogs, such as Beagles and Terriers, are prone to yapping because they were bred for their ability to chase or guard, and barking is sometimes part of the package. But all dogs can learn not to bark excessively or inappropriately. If you have a dog who is known for barking, nip the problem in the bud while the dog is still a pup.

Speak Up!

Sure, many dogs bark like crazy whenever they feel like it, but did you know that with a little training, your dog can actually be taught to do so on your command? Teaching your dog to speak when told is an excellent way to develop watchdog intuition. Teach your puppy to "Speak" by getting his attention with a treat or toy. Once he's excited over it, tell him in a bark-like way to "Speak!" Then, as soon as your dog lets out a woof, click him and give him the treat or toy so he recognizes that he has performed the desired task. Keep practicing this way, and your pup should catch on to "Speak" fairly quickly.

Once you recognize what sets your dog off into a barking frenzy, think carefully about how you can prevent these episodes from happening. The more barking your dog does, the more she gets reinforced for barking. (Remember, both positive *and* negative reactions reinforce behavior.) The more reinforcement a behavior gets, the more likely the behavior will reoccur and become stronger. If you want to have a quieter household, you need to short circuit as many of the things that trigger your dog's barking as possible.

Establish Reasonable Goals

A dog who barks a lot isn't just going to quit one day when you find a magic cure. Because barking is reinforcing to dogs, it often gets worse before it gets better. Confer with your family and set a reasonable goal for your dog. Maybe your dog is the type who barks when the doorbell rings; in this case, your goal might be that she's allowed to bark for thirty seconds and then she must listen when you tell her to be quiet. Or, if she hears a noise, she can let you know something's going on, but then she must stop barking and go to her bed. It really doesn't matter what the goal is, as long as it is simple and fairly easy for the dog to accomplish.

It is your job to discuss the problem, agree on a reasonable alternative, and then teach the solution to the dog. Don't be afraid to start with small goals and then increase the length of time the dog is required to be quiet by seconds. It isn't reasonable to expect a dog who has been barking excessively for years to stop overnight.

Find the Antecedents

An antecedent is the trigger or the cause of a behavior. For instance, if your dog barks at the sound of a knock or the doorbell, those things would be considered the antecedents for the behavior of barking. Knowing what triggers your dog's barking can be crucial to teaching her to be quiet. The pattern or chain of reaction goes like this: antecedent, behavior, consequence, appropriate behavior, reward. You need to complete this entire circuit of behavior in order to teach your dog not to bark excessively.

A good way to find antecedents is to keep a chart of when your dog barks and what happens right before she barks. Write down exactly what you think triggered the barking, then time how long it took her to stop and calm down. Once you do this, you will recognize when you are making progress in your training program and when you are spinning your wheels. You'll know you're on track if the number of seconds it takes your dog to calm down becomes fewer over time. Good dog trainers chart progress to see results!

Follow Through with Consequences

A consequence is similar to punishment, so alone it will only stop a behavior, because it doesn't teach the dog what she should do instead. For dogs who keep at it and barely take a breath between barks, you might want to use something to interrupt barking. If you stop the barking for a second, then you can reward him for being quiet. Some consequences that work effectively as interruptions include a squirt of water, a loud noise, shaking a can of pennies, or a nonelectric no-bark collar (this device is worn around the neck and distracts the dog by squirting a blast of citronella when she barks). Once you figure out how to get the dog to take a break from barking, plan in advance what the dog should do instead. This way, you'll be prepared and you'll know what behavior to reinforce.

▶ Hound mix barking

Notice the Right Stuff

Too often with a noisy dog, we tend to notice only when they are barking, and not when they are silent. Part of the solution for barking is acknowledging and reinforcing the dog when she is calm. Each time you reinforce quiet behavior, you're stockpiling money in the bank for a quieter dog overall. Pay attention to your dog at quiet times by petting or playing with him, giving him a treat, bringing him inside, letting him outside, opening the crate door, or whatever else might work at the moment. You'll notice that your dog will bark less over the course of several days or weeks (depending on the value of the reinforcement and the severity of the problem).

Set Up for Success

If you live in a busy neighborhood, be smart—letting your dog have unsupervised access to your yard is not a good idea. He will only find things to bark at, effectively reinforcing his obnoxious behavior. Poor management is money in the bank for more barking, because dogs think that barking is fun and will continue the behavior unless they have something better to occupy their time. Setting your dog up to succeed means that you use prevention to help your dog to be quiet, and then notice and reward him for *being* quiet. Following are some tips for setting your dog up to succeed.

Provide exercise. A dog can never have too much. Make sure your dog has plenty of fun activities, such as play dates with other dogs, and games of fetch, Frisbee, and hide-and-seek. Doggie day care, pet sitters, and dog walkers are other great options for exercising your dog when you're not around to do it yourself.

Pay attention. Be there to supervise and redirect your dog. When you are present in the yard, for instance, practice calling your dog away from what he is barking at and reward him for engaging in a different behavior.

Keep him busy. Dogs who bark are often big chewers, so make sure your dog has plenty of good stuff to chew. Try interesting toys, bones, and other treats that really let your dog exercise his jaws. Stuff hollow toys with peanut butter and dry dog food, and hide them all over the house and yard; this will give him something interesting to do while you are out.

Remove the antecedent. Prevent barking as often as possible by blocking his view with shrubs, closing the blinds, or rearranging the furniture. Not allowing your dog to practice the wrong behavior is more than half the cure.

Meet his needs. The more predictable your dog's routine, the better it is for him, so have a schedule and stick to it as much as possible. If you feed, walk, and play with your dog at predictable times, he will learn to trust you and feel secure.

Be ready. It is very important to be prepared to reinforce what's going right. The more you know what you want, the more likely you are to get it.

Use a marker signal. Using a clicker to help the dog to identify which behavior is rewardable (the quiet behavior) is crucial. This information is difficult to provide any other way, so always be ready with your clicker. Remember, the click marks the quiet behavior so you can then follow through with the reward.

Dogs Who Bark at Visitors

Dogs who go berserk when visitors enter your home might be overexcited, fearful, or downright aggressive. It's dangerous to attempt to train your dog to respond well to visitors while you are also trying to greet your guests. Your efforts probably won't be terribly successful, either. A new pattern of behavior is necessary to teach the dog to respond to visitors in a more appropriate way.

If your dog is aggressive or fearful of strangers, you should enlist a qualified professional dog trainer or behaviorist to help you evaluate your dog and correctly identify the problem. This person will also help you to set up training sessions that will enable your dog to learn better, safer greeting manners. The biggest task to tackle is changing your dog's attitude toward company. Here's a good way to accomplish that:

1. Put the dog out of the room and let your company come in and sit down.
2. After about ten minutes, let your dog out and have everyone ignore her.
3. Arm each person with the yummiest treats and have visitors drop those treats all around their feet.
4. Let your dog be the one to go to the visitor to take the treats.

Congratulations! You just made your first huge deposit for stopping barking at visitors. You might want to practice this scenario with your own family first, to teach the dog this new pattern of behavior and to help the family members learn a new way of managing the dog around company. Once you and your family have it down, repeat this as often as you can with lots of different people until your dog begins to look forward to having company at the door.

If you're not prepared to train your dog before a given occasion, put her in a separate room or in her crate when company arrives. You'll at least be removing her from the stimuli, and she won't fall back into her old behavior. This way, you won't lose ground by reinforcing her old patterns.

 Quick Fix: Strategic Placement
Being creative about changing your dog's environment might give you a little more peace and quiet. Think about planting a row of bushes in your yard, or close to the front blinds to block your dog's view of the neighborhood.

friendly options

Dogs who bark because they are happy to see company simply need a distraction to keep them quiet. Encouraging your dog to grab a stuffed animal on her way to the door is a perfect example of teaching her to do something that is incompatible with barking. It will keep her mouth busy, making it impossible for her to bark and hold the toy at the same time.

You'll want to make sure it's a toy she really loves so that she'll want to hold the toy more than she'll want to bark. You can even leave a basket of toys by the door and let your visitor select one to greet your dog with. This will teach your dog that visitors are fun but barking isn't part of that fun. Take advantage of any willing helpers such as neighbors, fellow dog lovers, and friends. The more your dog gets to practice greeting guests quietly, the better for everyone. Take your time and experiment with different toys to see which ones become your dog's favorites, and keep her so engrossed that she forgets to bark!

Taming Doorbell Madness

Dogs who burst into action at the sound of the doorbell need some help getting over this huge stimulus before they can be expected to be quiet. The sound of the doorbell ringing might be your dog's antecedent to barking, and the most difficult distraction for her. Most dogs with this problem explode into a cacophony of shrill barking and take several minutes to calm down.

The best way to manage these dogs is to teach them an alternative response to the ringing doorbell. The easiest—and noisiest—way to do this is through a process called "flooding." Flooding involves ringing the doorbell over and over when no one is there for the dog to greet so that eventually the ringing doesn't mean what the dog thinks it means. She will start to develop an alternative response to the doorbell and come to expect something different than what she originally thought.

You can also add a bit of classical conditioning to change the dog's association with the doorbell. Classical conditioning is about developing associations between a noise or object, in this case the doorbell, and something good, like a treat or a game of fetch. To incorporate conditioning into the training, ring the bell and shower the dog with treats or start throwing a ball around regardless of the dog's behavior (barking or not).

Here, unlike operant conditioning or clicker training, we are not requiring the dog to do something before she gets something. To the novice trainer, at first it might seem that we are rewarding the dog for barking when we ring the bell and treat the dog. In reality, we are forming an association between the doorbell and something good so that eventually instead of barking, your dog will be expecting a treat, a game, a toy, or a pat from the visitor. This can be a very powerful tool in trying to change your dog's association with doorbells. Using this technique might help to solve your barking problem faster than through other methods.

Dogs Who Bark for Attention

Some dogs have their owners all figured out. Remember that most dogs don't work for a living and have nothing else to do but sit around and watch you. They know just what to do to get what they want by barking at you until they get it. When a dog barks at you for attention, it usually means that he is confused about who's in charge in the family and might not have been taught enough rules and limits to give him a clue as to where he falls in the family hierarchy.

The one thing that almost always works for these needy, demanding dogs is to stop paying attention to them when they are barking and to start noticing, marking, and rewarding them for being quiet. Walk away, turn your head to the side, or turn your back on your dog to let him know that what he is doing is not rewardable. If your dog is used to getting his way by barking, this method of management might take a while, but overall it is a faster process and more productive than constantly yelling at the dog to be quiet.

Head Halters

There are several types of equipment you can use to shorten your training time by gently helping your dog to relax and trust that you are in charge. The Gentle Leader Headcollar is one such head halter. Head halters are an excellent investment, because with the proper introduction, they will cut your training time in half (see Chapter 8).

The original purpose of the head halter is to teach dogs not to pull, by guiding them under the chin. In essence, when a dog is wearing one of these you control his forward movement by controlling his head. The head halter has an added benefit, too: When fitted correctly, it puts gentle pressure on two points on the dog's head and neck, which helps relax the dog and makes him feel more secure.

Head halters should be introduced very slowly if they are to be a useful tool for you. Use lots of goodies as you are teaching your dog to wear the head halter, to create positive associations. The more positively you introduce your dog to this equipment, the more useful it will be to you. If you rush things, your dog's resistance will make the halter more of a hindrance than a help. However, once your dog is properly taught to wear the head halter and then learns to like wearing it, it can have an amazing effect on his behavior. Some dogs find the effect so calming that they become very mellow and actually forget to bark!

The Difference Between Operant and Classical Conditioning

Operant conditioning (click and treat) recognizes, and therefore encourages, desired behavior. Classical conditioning creates positive associations between two events.

Canine Massage

Canine massage is an often-overlooked, but successful, method of achieving a quieter dog. The massage technique most worthy of mention for changing unwanted behavior is called Tellington Touch, or T-touch. It was originally used on horses by a woman named Linda Tellington-Jones, but it has been applied to all kinds of animals for all kinds of behavior problems. (For more information on the T-touch technique, see Appendix for references.)

Dogs hold a lot of their emotions in their face and mouth area, and most dogs who are restless, tense, hyperactive, or aggressive tend to bark, chew, and bite to relieve anxiety. These animals can benefit from a bit of therapeutic massage on their muzzle and gum line.

The best T-touch technique involves making small circles on the muzzle and jaw line with the tips of the fore and middle fingers.

Lightly move the skin in a clockwise direction for a full circle, then pick your hand up and do another circle right next to it. Take your time, make each circle for a count of five, and remember to breathe.

You might want to start getting your dog used to this by sitting on a chair or the floor and having your dog sit between your feet. Use one hand for support under his jaw while you make circles with the other. The pressure should be light—about as much as would be comfortable if you made a circle on your eyelid. You can even slip your finger under the dog's lip and make small circles on the gum line itself. You might want to wet your fingers first if your dog has a dry mouth.

Hope for the Problem Barker

Barking doesn't have to be problematic for owners or neighbors. Owning a pet should be a rewarding experience, and barking should not get in the way of you and your family enjoying your pet. If you have an annoying barker, the time to act is now. The longer you let your dog reward herself by getting what she wants when she barks, the more barking you will have to hear.

Put together a training plan that will help reform your barking lunatic into the quiet companion you've always wanted. You have the tools to change the behavior; now it's time to get to work. Think about whether you are meeting your dog's basic needs for exercise, and change this if necessary. Increasing your dog's play-time with other dogs, for example, is often a huge factor in cutting down on barking. Most of all, don't give up. Even the most obnoxious barker can become a more enjoyable companion if he's taught to calm down. He just needs to be trained. Once you teach your dog to control his barking properly, then you can be sure that when he does bark, it's for a good reason!

7: Controlling a

Lots of dog owners routinely face the dilemma of stopping their rambunctious canines from jumping on people. Jumping is a natural dog habit, especially for young dogs and certain breeds, but there's no need to stop having visitors because the problem is so intense. You first need to understand why your dog jumps, and then teach him how to break the habit, so that he can function acceptably around people, both at home and in public.

Why Do Dogs Jump?

One reason why dogs jump is obvious: Jumping up on people works for dogs, because it's a fast way to get people to pay attention to them. Since dogs always do what works, the problem perpetuates itself to the point where a dog jumps constantly. But it's equally important to understand the lesser-known reasons—reasons that, once again, stem from their wolf ancestors.

Clearly, jumping is more than just the annoying, obnoxious behavior of dogs who can't control themselves. Young wolf cubs, when fed by older pack members, jump up, nip at, and lick the adults' muzzles. As young cubs grow, they continue to lick the muzzles of older superiors as a common form of greeting and respect, dogs have inherited this same behavior. Greeting each to face in this way also allows dogs to decide, after a few d sniffs, whether they have encountered a friend or foe, so they can proceed either to play or fight. And, when dogs have been away from their pack for a prolonged period of time, they use these behaviors once again, to re-establish their status within the group and find out where their family members have been.

Quick Fix: Just Walk Away
The absence of reinforcement for undesirable behavior can be a powerful message. Dogs expect the people they jump on to acknowledge them in some way. Train the people in your family to turn and walk away from your dog without any contact.

Needless to say, the long and short of it is that when pet dogs jump on us, they are trying to get close to our faces in order to greet us in a similar manner. Humans often unknowingly reinforce this instinctual jump-and-lick salutation when they hold young puppies up to their faces to hug and cuddle. These early experiences encourage a puppy's innate tendency to want to greet pack members—in this case, her human family—by jumping.

Although this natural behavior is a gesture of affection and happiness, it can easily scare or offend unknowing strangers—or owners. When people misunderstand jumping, it often results in the dog being isolated from the very people she is trying so hard to be with—an unhappy solution all around. But dogs who express their exuberance by jumping when they greet people need not be shut away from company. They just need to be taught appropriate manners around guests so that they can be part of family life.

The Welcoming Committee

People who place a lot of emphasis on stopping jumping are, in truth, barking up the wrong tree. It is far more effective to define what you prefer your dog to do instead, because, as already illustrated in previous chapters, you are more likely to reach your goal if you know what behavior you are looking for, and then reward your dog for performing it. For example, most people choose to have their dogs Sit and Stay when they say hello to people; this is a clear goal for the dog to accomplish and can be used in place of the jumping behavior. You should teach your dog how to Sit and Stay, and then reinforce it generously when she offers it around people, so that she learns this is the desired behavior.

Quick Fix: No Jumping Allowed

Many dog lovers don't mind if a dog jumps up when greeting them, but just because it's okay with your guest doesn't make it a good idea. Being consistent is a very important part of training, and you shouldn't send mixed messages to your dog by allowing him to jump on some people, but not others. Be clear about what the rules are and be a strong advocate for your dog. It is imperative that while you are teaching your dog an alternate behavior, no one, however well-meaning, sabotages the plan.

Build a History

Rewarding your dog over and over for sitting will make it more likely that he'll choose this correct behavior when faced with greeting new people. Remember, dogs do what works; if sitting is rewarded when he greets new people, he will try sitting as his first choice.

As you are teaching your dog not to jump by reinforcing appropriate behavior, also prevent your dog from practicing the wrong behavior as much as possible. Often, when guests or family members enter a house, they shower the dog with affection, but this only teaches the dog to jump up and act crazier. It's better to encourage visitors and members of your household to show self-control. Play, fun, and enthusiasm are important parts of well-balanced, bonded relationships for dogs, but these things should never be associated with people coming and going. Instead, practice calm arrivals by making it a habit to keep busy doing other things, without responding to your dog's prancing, barking, jumping, or panting. Then insist that guests and family members do the same.

Quick Fix: Jumping on Furniture

Many people allow their dogs on the furniture, and dogs love this, because furniture picks up people's scents, it's comfortable, and it usually affords dogs a better view of what is going on. The glitch is that the furniture picks up his scent, too. Be forewarned: Once you allow your dog on the furniture, it becomes his domain.

If your dog continues to sneak on to the furniture despite your disapproval, give her her own piece of furniture—a very comfortable dog bed.

Also, when a guest is visiting, keep a leash on your dog so that you can step on it whenever necessary to prevent jumping. Remember, stepping on the leash is a good management tool to use while you are teaching your dog a new behavior. Each time you fail to do this and your dog jumps on someone, you are putting money in the bank for this behavior and it will become stronger with time. Don't forget to keep a leash by your front door for quick access if unexpected visitors arrive. And keep your foot on your dog's leash anytime you go into the pet store or veterinary office, or you stop to talk to a neighbor on the street. The fewer opportunities your dog has to jump on people, the more swiftly she will learn to sit instead.

Click and treat the dog anytime she sits around company without being asked. For practice, ask a guest to go away and try to get your dog to sit again; this time, ask for Sit only once. If it happens, click and treat; if it doesn't, have the guest go away again. In this way, a dog learns by trial and error that if she wants the visitor to stay she must sit.

This exercise assumes that you have taught your dog to respond to the Sit command and you have practiced it in all environments with lots of distractions. Apply the Ten in a Row rule to see if your dog really knows how to Sit in each new environment. Do this by asking your dog to Sit ten times in a row without a click or treat (praise each correct repetition). If he doesn't get ten out of ten correct, you have more training to do. Go back to drilling and practicing amid this distraction until he can pass the test.

Self-control Exercise

Keep in mind that dogs don't learn self-control unless they are allowed to make choices and are rewarded for making good ones. The following exercise, Choose to Sit, is one example of helping your dog learn self-control so she will not jump on guests.

1. Greet visitors with the dog on a leash.
2. If the dog jumps, the visitor goes away.
3. If the dog sits, the visitor stays and the handler clicks and treats.
4. The dog learns by trial and error how to get the person to pay attention to him.
5. The handler supplies information by clicking and treating.
6. The visitor supplies consequences for not sitting by not allowing the dog to say hello to her.

As you try to solve your dog's behavior problems, keep this example in mind. Learning will last longer when the dog figures out on his own what the rewardable behavior is, especially if the dog is usually excellent in the absence of distractions but falls apart in public.

Provide opportunities to Practice

There is nothing like repetition to aid the learning process. The more opportunities the learner has to practice the desirable behavior and get rewarded for it, the more likely the learner is to offer this new behavior in real life. Short, interesting training sessions—with lots of changes in variables and delicious treats, toys, and games as rewards—will set you on the right track to having a dog who knows what to do and does it because you have taught him. Set up various training sessions where you practice different types of greetings, so your dog will gain the experience he needs to have good manners anywhere.

Many different things are happening when a dog is learning how to greet people without putting his paws on them. When training, change these variables slowly enough to maintain the dog's response to the command, but add enough variation to challenge him a bit. The more combinations of variables you train for, the more reliable your dog will be and the more likely he will be to offer a Sit/Stay instead of jumping. The key to having things run smoothly is not to change more than one variable at a time.

Every session will take you closer to your goal of a well-mannered pet. Some training scenarios that will teach your dog to be a polite greeter include:

- A person greeting you and your dog while you are out on a walk
- A visitor at the front door

- A person greeting your dog at the pet store, the vet, or the groomer
- A person with a dog greeting you and your dog
- A person sitting somewhere that you and your dog can approach
- A person walking up to you while you're sitting with your dog
- A child greeting your dog
- A person with food greeting your dog

Don't be afraid to go back and review Sit/Stay in places your dog has never been or places where he has a history of jumping and behaving obnoxiously. Start off in places where you can get your dog's attention easily, and gradually build up to places that are very distracting for him.

Mugging Company at the Door

Jumping is a problem most dogs do not outgrow. Dogs mainly jump because of their exuberance when greeting a person and welcoming them to play. Teaching your dog an alternate greeting behavior might be just the right solution. Here are some suggestions:

- Require a Sit/Stay or Down/Stay before people are allowed to pet your dog.
- Have your dog fetch a toy to keep his mouth busy and his feet off the company.
- Use a Go to Bed and Stay command to keep him away from the open door. This will not only prevent jumping on guests, it could also save your dog's life by keeping him away from any dangers outside.

Defining Your Dog's Greatest Distraction

Figuring out what makes your dog lose control in different environments will help you break training sessions down into smaller pieces, making it easier for your dog to be successful. It is important that you *do not* try to train your dog when she is totally out of control, because she isn't thinking about learning or paying attention at that point. Your training time will be more useful if you take it slowly and add one distraction at a time until your dog learns to ignore all distractions and stay focused on you instead.

Think about where you are likely to meet people when you are out on your walk. Does your dog go crazy when she meets new people while you are out? Are they passing you on the street or approaching you while you are sitting somewhere? Questions like these will help you to determine which scenarios distract your dog the most. For instance, many dogs find jumping irresistible not only when company arrives at the front door, but also when the kids come home from school, relatives visit, or other people with dogs walk by at the park. Defining the circumstances around which your dog loses control is useful, because it shows you where to start and what you will be working toward. Then, breaking the hardest distractions down into small training sessions that introduce one aspect of the distraction at a time will help your dog to learn a new response in a stimulating environment.

If your dog is out of control when people come to the door, for instance, one of your training sessions might start with practicing Sit and Stay in front of the closed door with no guest; then you could add a family member as the guest. Next, ask the family member to wait outside the door; then add a knock or the doorbell; eventually build up to practicing this with real guests.

If your dog is more likely to jump outdoors because he gets overexcited while playing ball, using a leash might help you manage this behavior while you reward him for doing something more appropriate instead. When your dog is excited, ask for Sit once. If he sits, click and throw the ball; if not, tell him "too bad" and walk away for a minute. Then try again after a couple of minutes. This way, a click marks the behavior of sitting on the first try, and the dog's reward is the toss of the ball. What better way to teach your dog self-control than to make throwing the ball dependent on his response to the Sit command?

The Bare Necessities
When it comes to learning not to jump, a dog will never be properly obedient if he hasn't first mastered basic training commands. You can't expect a dog who can barely handle Sit and Stay when there are no distractions to Sit and Stay when there are people around to jump on. If your dog has only a vague idea of what Sit and Stay mean, it is essential that you review these things with him somewhere quiet where there are few distractions.

Once he catches on, even a really energetic dog will love this game. Games such as this one are a great way to enrich your relationship with your dog while fine-tuning his response to basic obedience commands and general control issues.

Don't Punish Jumping

Sometimes it's especially tempting to use punishment when dealing with jumping because it seems to make the behavior disappear at first. In reality, punishment only stops the behavior temporarily; it does not instruct the dog to choose the right behavior, nor does it replace jumping with anything but the prediction of being punished. Another drawback is that emphasizing punishment as a response to jumping can backfire with sensitive dogs, making them suspicious, or afraid to greet people. On the other hand, dogs who have aggressive tendencies might actually turn and bite the person who is correcting them, creating a much more serious problem than the original one. Remember that punishment comes too late to teach the dog anything and, if poorly timed, might only teach your dog that visitors mean he's about to get punished. The best plan is to stick to teaching sitting in place of jumping. Make sure you notice him when he's not jumping; if you reward him with lots of attention, good behavior will be happening before you know it.

Quick Fix: Correcting a Climber

If you have a young puppy who jumps on counters, tables, or other furniture, you have probably given her too much unsupervised freedom too soon. It's important to distract your untrained puppy every time you catch her hopping onto things she shouldn't. One way to prevent this type of behavior while you're training your dog is startling her so that you interrupt the behavior. For example, rattle a shaker can with pennies in it, or clap your hands sharply. And remember, don't be afraid to keep your pup on the leash even while you're at home. This way, you can allow her to explore her surroundings but also step on her leash when she tries to jump on furniture.

Teaching Sit/Stay with Duration

To avoid jumping, you want your dog to Sit and Stay for an extended period of time. Extend the period of time slowly, until your dog will hold the position without trying to jump for one to two minutes. Eventually you'll also want your dog to perform this Sit/Stay despite distraction from other people or dogs.

Although you learned how to shape behavior for Sit/Stay in Chapter 4, take a moment to review it for these circumstances:

1. Use a treat to lure her nose upward and move your hand slightly back.
2. When her bottom hits the floor, click and treat.
3. Repeat this until your dog is offering Sit readily when she sees your hand above her head.
4. Practice without the treat in your hand. Click when her bottom hits the floor and follow up with a treat.
5. Put the treats away from your person and repeat, running with your dog to go get the treat after you click for her bottom hitting the ground.
6. Introduce distractions or train somewhere new and go back to the beginning if necessary.
7. Change the variables to mimic things that happen in real life: people visiting at the park, on the street, at the pet store, as well as at home.
8. Build duration in a nondistracting environment and increase it to double the amount of time you think you'll need. To build duration, simply count extra seconds between clicks and treats until your dog is easily waiting twenty to forty seconds for them.

Teaching your dog to maintain Sit/Stay for long periods of time will help you in public when there are lots of distractions. In practice you might be working on thirty seconds, while in real life your dog might give you only fifteen seconds, but it's a start. Even fifteen seconds will give you time to react quickly enough to prevent your dog from jumping on a visitor.

Creating a Sitting Maniac

It isn't hard to get a dog hooked on a behavior that works, but it does take time and thought along the way. One great activity to keep things interesting for puppies is the Sit for a Treat game. To play this game in a group-dog setting, take your dog off his leash and wander around the room greeting other puppies. Approach one of the other puppies with your dog and have the owner of the other puppy ask her dog to Sit, just once. If the pup sits on the first try, click and treat her, then move on to the next dog. If the puppy doesn't sit on the first try, simply walk away and ignore her, moving on to the next. Sometimes it takes a while for very energetic puppies to catch on, but it shouldn't be long before several pups are sitting perfectly in the middle of the room while the rest are running about wildly. Those one or two pups will refuse to move for anything, because they know what they need to do to get people to pay attention to them!

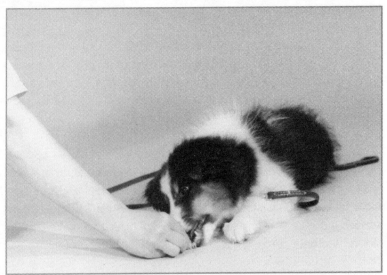

▶ Shetland Sheepdog puppy being lured into a Down

You can also play this game at home with your dog by inviting a group of family or friends over and having them wander around, armed with clickers and treats. Have your guests take turns giving only one command to Sit and then clicking and treating your dog for responding on the first try. You'll soon see your dog bouncing from person to person, sitting as fast as his rear end will let him, in order to earn his goody. Use your dog's dinner for this exercise if you'd like; it's a great way for him to practice his good manners and earn his dinner doing it.

Quick Fix: Visiting the Vet, Groomer, or Kennel

Experiences at these places are more pleasant when your dog is properly under control. Before entering, test and increase your dog's obedience by first walking around the grounds and taking your time as you enter the building, in order to familiarize your dog to the new surroundings and focus his attention. Hand him over to caretakers without fanfare and expect him to remain somewhat composed when he's returned to you. Any time you venture away from home, remember to treat the outing like a training session, not a vacation from obedience!

Jumping is a natural behavior gone astray through inappropriate reinforcement of the wrong behavior. There is nothing difficult about teaching your dog to Sit instead of jump; you just need to practice frequently, and in increasingly distracting environments, until your dog adopts it as second nature. Remember, as with any bad habit or addiction (yes, some dogs are so good at jumping they've become addicted to it), it takes time and patience to change unwanted behavior. Owning a dog who knows how to greet guests politely, without jumping, makes it easier to take him anywhere and have him actively involved in your life.

8: Leashing a Monster

Leash pulling is a frustrating—and common—problem with dogs. From the biggest Great Dane to the tiniest Chihuahua, all dogs, regardless of their size, learn from an early age to pull on their leashes to get where they want to go.

Leash pulling might not seem like a problem—until you walk around the block with a dog who thinks she's the lead in a sled team. It takes the fun out of a leisurely walk when one of your arms feels as though it is being pulled out of its socket. No wonder many people get so discouraged they stop taking their dogs for walks. Teaching your dog to walk with you properly is a time-consuming task, but it's well worth the effort, so stick to it.

The only Solution Is Training

If you look in pet stores and in catalogs, you will see dozens of devices that supposedly stop your dog from pulling. The truth of the matter is that dogs will pull until you teach them to stop, regardless of the equipment you are using. The key to any training program is *you*—how much time you invest in the project and how consistent you are about sticking to it until the job is done.

First off, it is important to define how you want your dog to behave on leash. Do you want her to walk at perfect heel position, or is a loose leash sufficient? Where exactly would you like your dog to be, and what will it look like when she's there? Will your arm be relaxed or extended, is sniffing okay, and which side should she be on? Decide now, so you'll be able to recognize what you need to reinforce and then reward it properly.

Leash Breaking for Puppies
To prepare your young pup for proper walks, put a buckle collar and lightweight leash on her for ten to thirty minutes, three times a day for a week. Allow her to drag it around the house or yard. Or, better still, attach the lead prior to playtime with another dog or a favorite toy. At first she might step on it, scratch her neck, refuse to move, or whine, but don't pay attention. Since many dogs like to chew the lead, you might need to spray it thoroughly before each session with a chewing deterrent such as Bitter Apple. Once your puppy is comfortable dragging the leash around, pick up the handle and coax her to walk on your left side by carrying and squeezing an interesting squeaky toy.

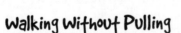

Walking Without Pulling

Leash walking behavior is not something that's going to change overnight. Teaching your dog to walk at your side rather than drag you requires practice and repetition. Remember, pulling works, or has worked, for a long time for most dogs. A huge step in the right direction is to stop following your dog when the leash is tight and she's pulling you. This might mean temporarily suspending walks so that she doesn't have the opportunity to practice pulling.

Managing your dog's behavior by not allowing her to practice it isn't teaching her to walk next to you, but it's a step in the right direction since she isn't being reinforced for the wrong behavior. Following are some tips for teaching loose-leash walking:

- Walk at a brisk pace and change direction frequently so that your dog has to pay attention to where you're going. The more you turn, the more your dog has to focus on you.
- Once you get the hang of walking and turning frequently, start to pay attention to the moment your dog turns to follow you, then click and treat him for catching up to you.
- At first, you might want to stop walking for a moment after the click so that the dog realizes what exactly he's getting clicked for. Use really delicious treats that your dog loves to keep his attention focused on you.
- Begin by practicing in a distraction-free place, and gradually go to busier places once your dog starts to understand.
- Attaching a six-foot leash to your waist will keep your hands free for this exercise, so you will be able to click and treat your dog when he is next to you. The message you are sending to your dog is that pulling does not get him where he wants to go because when he pulls in one direction it makes you go the other way.
- The faster you walk the better, since a steady pace forces dogs to pay attention to where you are going.
- Remember, the clicker is clearer and more precise than any other tool you can use to teach your dog what he's doing right. Using it to mark the behavior of being next to you will shorten your training time by half.

Since your dog has been pulling to get where she's going for as long as you've had her, the behavior is firmly established. To train her to choose to walk next to you instead, you will have to do lots of repetitions with particularly yummy rewards. The important thing is that the dog wants the reward more than she wants to pull. Be creative and fun, and your dog will soon be trotting happily next to you.

Quick Fix: On-Leash Games
Teaching your dog appropriate leash manners can be time consuming and tedious. Remember to break up walking sessions with some fun ideas. Try playing the targeting game as you walk by having your dog touch your hand or pant leg with her nose, and don't walk a long distance without changing direction or stopping frequently to make your dog Sit. These techniques are excellent ways for your dog to learn to control his enthusiasm while you are teaching him to walk properly on the leash.

Adding Duration to Your Walks

Once your dog catches on to getting clicked for coming back to your side, raise the criteria by training him to stay there for a step or two before you reward him. Eventually, build the length of time the dog must walk next to you for several minutes, until he's no longer inclined to pull. Practice having him walk with you for different lengths of time around a variety of distractions, until he sticks close under any circumstance.

Changing the Variables

Practicing proper leash walking skills in a new environment—with people, dogs, cars, bicycles, and other distractions—is critical to the reliability of this behavior. To help your dog to learn to stay with you despite distractions, change one variable at a time. There are two major variables involved in teaching your dog to heel: the distance to the distraction and the intensity of the distraction (this has to do with speed, noise level, and quantity). By controlling the variables and working slowly to introduce distractions while you maintain your dog's ability to heel, you will teach your dog to walk nicely on a leash regardless of the distractions around her.

Keep in mind that if you can't get your dog to perform the behavior, you are probably too close to the distractions and she can't concentrate. Back away from the action until you reach a point where your dog will perform the behavior well. Then, once your dog can handle it, bring her closer to the action. Here are some reminders to set your dog up for success.

- Reduce the intensity of the distraction (quieter, slower, less of it) as needed.
- Use your best treats; training is difficult, so make it worth his while.
- Offer a high rate of reinforcement in a new environment.
- Click and treat less frequently when the dog starts to perform the behavior reliably, for longer periods.

Common Distractions

The type of distractions you are working around is a huge consideration when you are teaching your dog to walk on leash properly. Following are the three major categories of distractions:

1. **Things that move.** These are the things that incite your dog's prey drive—her desire to chase after cars, bikes, squirrels, runners, dogs, motorcycles, balls, or kids. Every dog has a different level of distractibility, but most dogs find things that move irresistible.
2. **Things that smell.** The majority of dogs are motivated most of all by their stomachs, and for the hunting breeds especially, the "nose to the ground" behavior can be quite

a challenge. Examples are food, animals, other animals' feces, and wildlife.

3. **Things that make noise.** Some dogs are more sensitive to sound than others. The average dog will get over it quickly and learn to ignore sounds if you change the variables, distance, and intensity slowly.

Whatever the distraction, it's important to pay attention to your dog's excitement level and tone things down when necessary, so that he is able to absorb the lesson and learn properly.

Quick Fix: The Element of Surprise

Hide rewards all around your training area before you start your leash-walking session. It will be a huge surprise to your dog when she is unexpectedly rewarded with a delicious treat or an awesome toy that you pull out of the bushes. By hiding goodies everywhere, you'll hold your dog's attention and keep her guessing about what you're going to pull out next. This element of surprise will make you far more interesting to your dog, and it will make her much more willing to learn to walk with you.

The Mule Impersonator

Slow-poke pups can be as tough to teach as distracted, hyper dogs when it comes to leash walking. Laggards often plant their butts and will not budge, even with coaxing or cooing. There are several tricks you can use to get these dogs to follow you:

1. Put tension in the lead but don't pull. Make sure the leash is hooked to a regular collar, not a training collar.
2. As soon as your dog takes a step toward you to steady herself, be ready to click, treat, and lavish with praise.

3. Repeat this every time your dog stops. Don't go back to her; simply ignore the wrong behavior and pay attention to the right one instead.

4. Within ten minutes or so most dogs give up their stubborn-mule impression and go with you. However, some dogs might need several sessions before they give up, so remember to be patient.

Training Equipment

Training collars, head halters, leashes, and other devices are just that: devices. Their purpose is to manage pulling while you are teaching your dog to heel. The goal is for your dog to learn to heel with the help of training devices and then ultimately heel on her own whenever you ask her, even when not on leash.

Never Go Unleashed

Dogs are impulsive and love to chase things that run, so be cautious about giving your dog freedom in unfenced areas. Your dog might be the best-trained canine in the neighborhood, but if a cat runs across the street, he's still likely to follow. Use a leash on all walks on city streets and be careful when allowing off-leash freedom.

You must teach your dog the step-by-step process for heeling before you start using the device itself. After the dog has learned how to get rewarded, using a training device will help you sort out various distractions. Be prepared that in special situations, such as a trip to the veterinary clinic, you might need to use some extra management before your dog is completely trained.

Collars

Slip collars are useful tools when it comes to teaching dogs proper leash etiquette. The main varieties include:

Chain slip collars: The slip collar restricts the dog's airway for a fraction of a second, making it unpleasant to pull. For quick slide-and-release action, use a slip chain with flat, small links. It should be ½ to 2 inches larger than the thickest part of your dog's skull; snug collars deliver timelier corrections. This type of collar stays in place better when properly positioned—high on the neck, behind the ears, with the rings under the dog's right ear.

Make sure the active ring (the one the leash attaches to) comes across the top of the right side of your dog's neck, so the slip collar will loosen properly after corrections.

Nylon slip collars: Neither round nor flat nylon slip collars offer the slide-and-release action of a chain, but they do deliver stronger corrections than buckle collars. As with any collar, the nylon slip should only be tightened momentarily while correcting; constant tension means the dog isn't being told when he's doing well and when he's doing poorly.

Another variation that operates on a similar principle is the pinch collar: Rather than slip action, this collar works by pinching the skin around the dog's neck.

One word of caution: If the collar used for training is different from the one your dog usually wears, he probably won't obey well when he isn't wearing his training collar. Be prepared to enforce all your commands consistently at all times, so he'll behave regardless of which collar he's wearing.

The Exercise Connection

Nowhere is lack of exercise more apparent than when a dog is on leash. A dog with few outlets for his energy will pull, spin, and tug on leash to get where he wants to go. Giving your dog appropriate outlets for his energy, such as romping with other dogs, swimming, and playing fetch, will help him to be calmer on the leash. Don't forget that active dogs need at least thirty minutes to an hour of flat-out running a day, to take the edge off of their energy. Without this outlet, expect behavior problems.

The Benefits of Head Halters

No one device is right for every dog, but the head halter is the most useful for most dogs, particularly if they are large and strong, and you could use some extra help controlling them. The head halter works by pulling the dog's head downward, making it impossible to walk until the dog stops pulling. Head halters don't hurt your dog at all. In fact, they're great if your dog's trachea or esophagus is sensitive to pressure; they allow for tremendous control, without irritation.

One particular name brand of head halter, the Gentle Leader Headcollar, tends to fit better than others. It has two adjustable straps: one for the neck and one for the muzzle. The leash clips underneath the dog's chin. Think of the way a halter on a horse fits and you'll have an idea of how this works. The head halter controls the dog's forward movement by controlling her head. You would never expect to move a horse by pulling on its neck, but you can easily move a 1,200-pound animal in any direction by guiding it by its head—well, at least most of the time!

This same principle works for dogs. The head halter is not a muzzle—the dog can eat, catch a ball, and bite with it on, and no dog should be left unattended while wearing it. If your dog tries to bite or eat something he shouldn't while wearing the head halter, close his mouth by gently pulling up on the leash. The pressure will push his head down, preventing him from continuing the behavior.

Introduce the head halter gradually, over a period of two weeks. Slowly teach your dog that wearing it is fun and means good stuff is about to happen. The more time you take to make this fun, the more useful it will be. Your goal is to make him as excited to see the head halter as he is to see his leash. Using a clicker and the yummiest treats, introduce the head halter by following these steps:

1. Show the halter to your dog and click and treat her for sniffing at it.

2. Open the nose loop and click and treat your dog for poking her nose through it to get at the treat.

3. Once she's eagerly putting her nose through the loop on her own, give her a good-sized treat; while she's chewing, fasten the neck strap.

4. Let her move around a bit and click and treat her for not pawing at her nose.

5. If your dog gets the nose loop off, take the whole thing off and leave her alone for about ten minutes. Completely ignoring her will make her all the more eager to work with you again. The idea here is that she will want to keep the halter on because you pay extra attention to her and give special treats only when she has it on.

6. Later, when she isn't pawing as much, attach a leash to the clip under the chin and repeat steps 4 and 5. Click and treat her for walking without pawing at her face every time you introduce a new distraction or variable.

7. You are now ready to use the head halter on your walks, but go slowly. Take your dog for a short walk, and click and treat her for walking outside without pawing at her face. Make sure the walk is no more than five minutes long.

8. As your dog gets used to wearing the head halter in public, you can gradually increase the distractions, the length of time you walk her, and any of the other variables.

The head halter can be a wonderful tool for helping you manage your dog around distractions and teaching her not to pull, but introducing it takes time, so don't rush your dog. If dogs have problems with the head halter, it's usually because their owner rushed the introduction as soon as the dog seemed to tolerate the halter fairly well.

Make sure you read the halter's directions carefully before you use it on your dog. It's important that you teach your dog to wear it properly—don't let him lunge or pull. Be patient during this intro-duction. The head halter is more useful if you let the dog learn to like wearing it. If you still have trouble, after a week or two, find a qualified positive trainer to help you.

Walking a Scared Dog

Any dog can be trained to walk at heel, and frightened dogs are no exception. It's best to teach these dogs how to deal with novel noises in order to build their confi-dence before you try to teach them to walk on the leash. Once scared dogs overcome their skittishness, then you can teach them to heel around distractions.

Lunging and on-Leash Aggression

Teaching your dog good on-leash behavior does more than make your time walking together enjoyable. Sometimes, aggressive behavior in adult dogs gets its start from inappropriate leash training as a young puppy. If you learn some basics about dog social interaction, however, you can prevent aggression.

For instance, adult dogs often find it rude when an adolescent dog jumps on them or makes an uninvited move into their space. When dogs are off leash and encounter other dogs—or any other stimuli—they are free to decide what to do. They can choose to get away, give off a "don't bother me" attitude, or invite the other dog to play. Dogs on leash cannot show these same emotions, and this causes them to feel more cornered and threatened.

The human holding the other end of the leash often makes the problem worse by not paying attention to what the dog is doing and making the leash too short. Tightening the leash doesn't help, because it signals to the dog that trouble lies ahead.

owner Manners

People with on-leash dogs tend to approach each other head-on, whereas dogs normally approach each another in a curved half circle. For dogs, approaching head-to-head is a combative signal that you might want to fight. Typically when encountering each other, one dog might recognize another dog's rank and lower himself slightly to signal that he means no harm. Humans, however, often pull the leash up when another dog approaches. Pulling up on the leash changes your dog's body posture into a more threatening stance, causing the other dog to react and your dog to become defensive. Then, a higher-ranking dog, when taken by surprise, might attack your dog for posturing the wrong message at the last minute. No wonder it is difficult for on-leash dogs to get along!

By inadvertently pulling the dog into a more dominant posture, the human is responsible for the greeting gone wrong. This comes down to poor leash manners on the dog's part, and not enough understanding or control on the owner's part. Teach your dog to be polite on leash around other dogs by clicking and treating for approaching sideways instead of head-on, turning his head away instead of staring, and staying low and not jumping on the other dog.

Dog Manners

Dogs who, in play, launch themselves at other on-leash dogs are also sending the wrong message. A rude dog such as this is breaking the cardinal rule: no jumping on an adult dog. It's especially bad manners to jump on dogs who are trapped on leash and can't get away! Dogs who do this are often corrected sharply by other dogs, and their owners mistake this for true aggression. If this scenario is repeated enough, the friendly dog learns to be defensive; this is the beginning of leash aggression.

No on-leash dog should have to put up with another dog jumping on him, even in play. It is important as the owner of your dog to make sure that you have appropriate control of your dog around other dogs. The more well-trained your dog is, the better he will be accepted by other on-leash dogs, and people as well.

▶ **Golden Retriever takes German Shepherd for a walk**

Hot to Trot

Always be sure there isn't a physical reason why your dog won't walk with you. Check his feet for cuts, make sure the pavement isn't too hot, and watch that salt-treated roads don't sting his feet in the wintertime.

The head halter is a must for teaching on-leash manners. When used correctly, this device will not only prevent lunging and jumping, but also lower the dog's head and body carriage, which will make him less likely to provoke other dogs.

Using the Leash Properly

The best leash for walking an aggressive dog is a six-foot nylon or leather leash. A dog with lunging or aggression problems should not be on an extendable leash, nor should she ever be off leash around other dogs. A six-foot leash allows you to control your dog and keep her close. (Use a leather leash ¼-inch wide for dogs up to 15 pounds, ½-inch wide for dogs 16–45 pounds, ¾-inch wide for dogs 46–75 pounds, and 1-inch wide for dogs over 76 pounds.)

The way you hold the leash is important to your dog's progress as well. It's generally best to hold it with two hands, one hand through the loop end and the other about halfway down the length. This allows your dog a little slack but not so much that she can lunge ahead of you without you being able to prevent it easily. Never hold the leash so tightly that your dog barely has enough room to move. The slacker the leash is (without letting her get too far ahead of you), the less confined and cornered she will feel when she sees another dog. When the leash is attached to a Gentle Leader Headcollar, remember that it is self-correcting and does not require you to jerk or pull.

Before your dog lunges, try to get her attention back on you by moving in the opposite direction. Make sure you are prepared not only to move away from the other dog, but also to click and treat your dog when she moves with you.

Quick Fix: Avoid Confrontation
Increase your dog's willingness to turn away from other dogs by throwing a handful of treats in the grass so he has to hunt them up. The time it takes for him to do this will give the other dog and owner time to go by you. Then, when your dog finishes simply continue on your walk.

Leash Manners

For dogs with good social skills who get into trouble when on leash, take some simple steps to improve on-leash manners. First of all, you need to use the right equipment. There are lots of products on the market that help you to control pulling. The problem is, these devices fool you into thinking your dog knows not to pull on his leash, but as soon as the device is removed, the dog goes back to pulling. Keep in mind that all training collars facilitate training, but they do not replace it.

Most people make the mistake of putting the training collar on their dog and then expecting the dog to figure out magically what she is supposed to do. As with any other training, if you don't reward the dog for walking with you, the dog will have no idea what is expected. Most dogs who are not rewarded for the appropriate behavior simply run to the end of the leash, get a yank from their owner, go back to her side for a moment, and then quickly end up running to the end of the leash again. Not all dogs respond this way, however. Some very sensitive dogs fall apart the first time they are corrected. These dogs might never try to pull again, but they are doing so out of fear, not because they have learned that you want them to walk next to you. Sensitive dogs should probably not wear a training collar. They learn quicker through gentler methods, such as the halter. The halter collar fits over the back of the neck and top of the muzzle, which mimics what a mother dog does when she disciplines her pups. In this way, many dogs learn to trust their handlers and pay more attention to them, rather than fear them.

Teaching Your Dog to Leave It

This command will help tremendously when stopping your dog from being aggressive or lunging at another dog or person. It will also help you in other situations, such as preventing your dog from chasing a cat or squirrel across a busy street. Leave It means teaching a dog to stop what she's doing, or thinking about doing, and look back at her handler. Once your dog is looking at you, you have a greater chance of getting her to respond to further directions. Leave It is the most important thing your dog must learn if she is going to be safe to walk in public places. The faster and more reliably she responds, the better your control will be.

The longer you can get your dog to look at you, the more you will be able to control him around other dogs and people. When teaching Leave It, it is important to catch the dog before he starts to lunge and bark. Once he starts, he is no longer in learning mode, and no amount of yelling or corrections will get him there. Beat him to this highly charged emotional state by interrupting him before he really notices the other dog. Then reverse direction so that he moves with you, and click and treat.

If your timing is off, and you don't turn him in time, he will explode into a frenzy of barking. There is nothing you can do at this point; just get through it and try again the next time. Above all, don't yell at or correct the dog, or else you'll reinforce the undesirable behavior. The good news is, with enough practice and repetition, your dog might eventually start to offer this behavior on his own!

Here are the steps to teaching your dog to leave another dog:

1. Use familiar dogs at first so that you can completely control your training session. Have your helper and "distraction dog" start on the opposite side of the street.
2. Make sure you interrupt your dog when he's thinking about lunging or barking. Interrupt him by saying his name and then turning 180 degrees in the opposite direction. Click and treat him for turning with you.
3. If your dog doesn't turn with you, it means that you are too close to the distraction dog; move away and try again.
4. Throw a handful of goodies for him to clean up after you click so that you make it well worth his while to pay attention to you.
5. Once your dog is ignoring the other dog and turning with you easily, shorten the distance by having the dog approach on the same side of the street and repeat steps.
6. Build up to being able to have the distraction dog pass within several feet with no reaction from your dog.
7. Switch distractions, using different dogs and changing where you practice until your dog ignores any dog anywhere.

Lack of Socialization

So far, you've read about dogs who have fairly good social skills but poor leash manners. What about dogs who have not been socialized with other dogs? Dogs who lack social experience are a more serious problem. Dogs with social skills know that not all dogs are going to attack them, because they have had good experiences with other dogs. But dogs who have not been socialized with other dogs have nothing to go on; therefore, every dog they see, friendly or not, is perceived as a threat.

Puppies must be socialized to be around other dogs between eight and eighteen weeks of age. If not, they will never be socially normal with other dogs. Socialization is like training, however: It must be fostered and maintained. If dogs don't practice their social skills, they lose them. Dogs need to play with others of their own kind to learn acceptable behavior and appropriate body language. Without these experiences they begin to act suspiciously and aggressively toward other dogs. Most people notice this problem is worse on leash, when the dog feels trapped and can't escape.

Don't Push It

Dogs with few or no social skills are never going to be totally friendly or trustworthy with other dogs. There is no such thing as resocializing an adult dog who's had no experience with other dogs. Doing so can be dangerous and might end in injury to dogs or the humans who interfere. Acknowledge that though you would like your dog to get along with other dogs, your dog is content not to have any contact with them. Don't force your own desire for your dog to have friends; she might feel she has as many friends as she needs, and no amount of pushing on your part will change that. Respect what your dog is trying to tell you and keep her safe around other dogs by teaching her to respond to Leave It.

The Bar Is open, the Bar Is closed

This technique uses the principles of classical conditioning to change the way your dog feels about other dogs on leash. The presence of other dogs means that the bar is open and all kinds of good things happen, including affection, attention, and treats, regardless of the dog's behavior. (He can be lunging or barking hysterically, yet you continue to drop treats like it is Christmas.) Then, when the other dog disappears, so do the treats, games, and attention.

Classical conditioning attempts to change the way the dog feels about having other dogs around by associating other dogs with good things. The drawback is that it takes the animal time to recognize the association. Practice this method frequently, to give your dog an increasingly big bank account for responding positively when encountering other dogs. Eventually your dog will like having other dogs around because it means that he is going to have access to all the things he loves.

Here's how it works in real life:

- Choose a spot where other dogs are likely to pass by and bring all of your best reinforcements.
- When other dogs are within sight, regardless of your dog's behavior, the bar is open. You bounce the ball, throw it, roll it, and shower your dog with treats, toys, and attention. As soon as the dog is out of sight, the bar is closed. You put your goodies away, step on the leash, and ignore your dog completely for at least two minutes.
- When another dog comes by, open the bar again; when he disappears, the bar is closed.
- After repeating this over and over again your dog is going to learn to react better to other dogs!

Leash-pulling and on-leash aggression are serious problems. These behaviors won't go away with just a little training; good leash behavior needs to be constantly maintained. Remember, dogs revert back to old habits if you don't consistently reinforce the right behaviors. With time, patience, love, and training, however, you can teach any dog to walk well on the leash, without displaying any signs of aggression to people or other dogs!

9: Discouraging a Digger

Does your backyard look like an archaeological dig? Some dogs dig huge craters that resemble dirt swimming pools, while other canine archaeologists prefer to leave dozens of smaller holes conducive to ankle breaking. Regardless of your dog's digging style, most dogs find this activity pleasurable and self-rewarding, and once they get going it can be hard to stop them. Unfortunately, digging is practically the only problem that cannot be prevented, lessened, or solved with obedience training (although training sometimes indirectly reduces the behavior because it engages your dog mentally and physically). You'll have to introduce some other creative strategies to beat your pooch's urge to excavate anywhere and everywhere.

Why Do Dogs Dig?

Dogs don't dig because they are dominant, belligerent, unaware of authority, or out of control—they do it instinctually, to make a comfortable place to lie down or to make a nest-like den for their puppies. Plus, of course, interesting smells in the soil and the wonderful feeling of dirt on their toes when they are vigorously burrowing are hard for any dog to resist. For some dogs, the instinct to dig is particularly strong. Most of the Terrier breeds, for example, were bred to dig out mice, rats, moles, and other vermin. Generally, however, dogs also dig for a variety of other emotional or physical reasons, ranging from boredom, frustration, and lack of exercise, to a real need to stay cool on a hot day. Looking at some of the reasons for digging might help you to get to the bottom of your dog's digging problem.

Boredom

A bored dog is a ticket to destruction. A dog with nothing to do will bark, howl, chew, destroy, and dig. Digging is a great stress reliever, and unearthing whatever treasures a dog can find is well worth her effort. If you think that boredom might be your dog's motive for digging, take steps to improve her environment now. Give your dog lots of different safe, fun toys. Take her for a romp in the woods, play with other dogs at the park, or teach her tricks. Any new stimulation you add to her routine will help to alleviate some of the boredom that is causing her to dig. In addition to physical exercise, mental exercise is another great way to alleviate a dog's boredom. Here are some ideas for fun physical and mental workouts:

- Stuff Kong toys (rubber, cone-shaped toys with a hollow middle for treats) with peanut butter and let your dog figure out how to get the food out. You can also put peanut butter or cream cheese on the inside of the shaft of a marrow bone (uncooked). Either way, your dog will have a blast licking it out.
- Freeze the toy to make this an even cooler challenge on a hot day.
- Invite a friend's dog to spend the afternoon playing and wrestling with your dog.
- Buy interesting toys for your dog and rotate them weekly so that your dog always has something new to play with.

- Hide treats in all different places in the yard for your dog to find.
- Put your dog's meals in a treat-dispensing toy and let him work for his dinner.
- Make some agility equipment—tunnels, ramps, jumps, etc.—and teach your dog to negotiate them with and without your help.

Remember that dogs need a variety of play, training, and exercise to be happy, healthy, and content family pets. When any behavior is extreme, like digging or barking, it usually is an advertisement that your dog needs more of something. In most cases it's that the dog is bored and distressed because she does not get enough exercise or one-on-one time with her owner.

▶ **Golden Retriever, ready to dig in**

Quick Fix for Digging
If your dog tries to dig out of the yard, you might want to bury ¼-inch mesh wire along the fence line to make it impossible for her to dig past a certain depth. Most dogs get discouraged once they hit something that won't let them dig any deeper, and find other pursuits.

frustration

If your dog is unsupervised in a fenced yard or dog pen, he might begin digging out of frustration. Just think how aggravating it must be for a dog who can see and hear people passing by, but can't get to where the action is. A dog who is frustrated because he has been confined for too long will often try to dig his way to freedom. Keep an eye on your dog when he's in the yard, and stimulate his environment by following some of the above suggestions, such as hiding toys packed with his dinner or peanut butter, or hiding bones and things to chew in the area where he is confined. The best way to alleviate frustration is to spend more time with your dog and provide him with more things to think about and do. Get outside and play with him, and then distract him from digging if he does it while you are present.

Exercise

If there is one thing that can save you time in the long run, it's providing your dog with enough exercise. The more opportunities your dog gets to run, chase, swim, wrestle, roll, and romp, the less energy she has to dig holes. We've already established that all dogs need at least thirty or more minutes of exercise a day, but if you own an active dog—and most diggers are very active—she will need at least one to three hours of exercise daily. Whether you take her for long runs in the woods, allow her off-leash time to play with other dogs, or enroll her in a doggie day care program, she needs activity. Make sure you're doing what you can to meet her basic needs before you complain about the digging.

Provide Shade

Not paying attention to a dog's basic need to be cool on a hot day can also contribute to your dog's digging problem. When it's hot, a dog's instincts tell him to find a cool, dry place to rest. Often, in the absence of adequate shade, a dog's natural way of cooling himself is to dig a hole and lie in it. If your dog is outdoors in hot weather, provide plenty of shade, shelter, and water, or consider leaving him indoors with the air conditioning on or a fan running. All dogs have a different sensitivity to heat and cold; observe your dog for signs that it's too hot or too cold for him outdoors. Here are some ideas for keeping cool on a hot day:

- Pop your dog's peanut butter-stuffed Kong in the freezer, for a chilly treat.
- Set up a beach umbrella and a kiddie wading pool in the yard. This is especially great for dogs who love the water, like Labrador Retrievers.
- Put some ice cubes in his water bowl.
- Freeze some dog biscuits in water and put them in the wading pool.
- Get a special sun-reflecting tarp and secure it over your dog's outdoor pen.

For the sake of his comfort—and health—you need to provide your dog with plenty of water and shade on hot days. Make sure that even an active pooch is not allowed to overdo it with play and exercise. Try taking your dog out for exercise early in the morning or after the sun goes down to prevent heat stroke.

Quick Fix: Filling Existing Holes

There are many theories regarding what to do about the holes that your dog has already dug in your yard. Some people leave the holes alone and then the dog only digs in the holes he's made. Other people put large rocks in the existing holes before filling them in. Another effective way to stop your dog's digging is to bury some of her poop in each hole. This way, when she uncovers it, she'll think she's found something she's already buried before. Then she'll be more inclined to leave the spot alone. Experiment and see what works best for your dog.

Setting Up a Legal Digging Zone

Dogs whose genetics tell them to dig need alternative outlets for their enthusiastic escapades. Replacing the inappropriate behavior with a more appropriate one is the only permanent solution. If digging comes naturally to your dog, why not provide a safe, legal place for him to dig by making a digging pit. A digging pit can be any size, but 4 feet x 4 feet for small dogs and 8 feet x 8 feet for larger breeds is a good general guideline. Use garden timbers to build a box shape and fill the box with sand. You might actually want to dig out the existing soil and make a bed of stone for the bottom to supply good drainage. This way, it won't become a mud puddle in inclement weather. Fill the rest of the pit with the type of play sand used in children's sandboxes, and then distribute the sand evenly. If your dog stays in a chain-link run while you're away during the day, you might also want to make a second, smaller pit out of a child's sandbox, so she can still have a good time digging while you're not home.

Now comes the fun part! Once you've built your sandbox,

bury toys, treats, balls, and other surprises for your dog to find. Make some of the treasures easy to locate, others more difficult. The more of a digger your dog is, the more challenging you should make the treasure hunt. Periodically (once a week), hide new treasures and rake the pit to remove any old cookies, bones, or other treats. Be creative in what you bury and your active dog will know exactly where to dig to find the good stuff. Here are some ideas for buried treasure:

- Hard dog cookies
- Kongs stuffed with peanut butter and treats
- Marrow bones (real ones from the butcher, uncooked is safest)
- Rawhide sticks, bones, and chips
- Pig's ears smeared with cream cheese inside a paper bag
- A small cardboard jewelry box filled with treats
- A cardboard ice-cream box with treats or a chew toy inside
- A favorite toy, such as a ball or a stuffed animal, hidden in a paper bag

Whatever the treasure, be sure it is something that your dog can safely have while unattended. Experiment while you are watching him to be sure he doesn't eat anything that he shouldn't (like the paper bag that you've hidden the tennis ball in). A certain amount of shredding is fine, you just don't want him eating the entire empty ice-cream container!

Maintaining Your Doggie Sandbox

You might want to invest in a metal rake so that you can clear any uncovered treasure from the digging pit and keep the sand loose and inviting. Also remember to add fresh sand periodically, to provide plenty of places to hide new goodies.

Regardless of the solutions you choose to distract and discourage a canine archaeologist from turning your yard into the Grand Canyon, the only real way to stop a digger for good is not to give him the opportunity to dig in inappropriate places. Correcting digging is an ongoing process—remember, you aren't fighting your dog; you're fighting nature. This means you'll have to monitor your dog more closely than the Secret Service guards the president. Supervise him constantly, don't leave him unattended in the yard for extended periods of time, and consider building him a digging area of his own. A dog who really enjoys digging will respond well when he sees he has a place to practice it free and clear.

You'll notice that there are no suggestions here regarding punishment. Excessive digging is a symptom of a larger problem. Digging is the dog's way of releasing pent up energy, boredom, and frustration. Instead of punishing your dog, make up for what she is lacking and alleviate her boredom by signing her up for fun classes that teach her obedience, tricks, or agility. Be sure to give her lots of stimulating toys that she doesn't see every day. Be creative in providing lots of exciting activities for your dog, and soon you'll be seeing a lot fewer holes in your backyard.

10: Reclaiming a Runaway

Are you tired of dealing with a wayward dog who bolts out the back door or slips out through the gate any chance he gets? Dogs who don't come when they are called can be exasperating, but it helps to understand they probably act this way because they've learned that getting away from you is somehow rewardable. If they run off and find things to eat, roll in, and play with, for example, then taking off has huge benefits, leaving them with little incentive to come and be with you.

Why Do Dogs Run Away?

When the average person calls her dog, she typically throws the leash back on and heads home, crates the dog, and then goes to work, or puts the dog in the car and drives away. Through situations like these, dogs learn that coming to their owners normally isn't beneficial, because their owners don't provide rewarding consequences. No wonder lots of dogs choose to reward themselves by running away!

The difference between a trained dog who comes when called and an untrained dog who doesn't is based on the dog's perception of who controls what he wants. Dogs behave in ways that benefit them, so the key to having a dog who is always willing to come when called is making it worth the dog's while, regardless of other distractions. Trained dogs know that their owners hold the keys to everything they want, and that they must do something to get it.

Using a Leash to Control the Variables

The most important thing to remember is that every time your dog takes off and has a good time she is putting money in her bank account for not coming back. Don't allow an untrained dog to roam off leash in an unsafe area or an area where she will be diffi-cult to catch. A dog who has an unreliable recall is a danger to her-self. She doesn't have good judgment and will often run in the street, get lost, or eat something harmful. If you love your dog and want to keep her safe, use a leash in unfenced areas so that you do not give your dog the opportunity to run away.

Keeping your dog on leash also gives her the ability to be right more often and allows you to reinforce those choices, making it more likely she will choose you again and again. Don't use the leash to force her to come by yanking on it. Instead, use it merely to limit her options and teach her the best choice. This way, you will make it more likely that she will choose to come back to you instead of running toward a distraction. Then, when you eventu-ally reach the point where you are ready not to use a leash any-more, you will be able to make the transition easily and maintain the same level of behavior.

Making Rewards Worth the Effort

Your dog needs rewards if he's going to choose coming to you over pursuing a distraction. Remember that a squirrel, cat, child, or another dog is a thrill to chase, bark at, or sniff around. If your dog chooses to be with you over another distraction, make sure you have the best treats, toys, or games ready as rewards. When teaching Come, the most important thing to do first is get your dog to turn in your direction. Once she does look at you, you need to mark your dog's good behavior with a click, followed by a treat, a game, or an opportunity to interact with the distraction—but only after checking in with you first. Using rewards in this way is not a bribe; you are simply requiring that your dog check in with you before he gets what he wants. For most dogs, learning this game almost completely eliminates the desire to run away. Using rewards in this way is great for showing your dog that you control access to what he wants and you pay up when he checks in with you.

▶ **Hound mix wearing a gentle leader**

Ideas for Rewards

Using a variety of exciting rewards will enhance your dog's performance and make the process of teaching him to come all the more fun. Keep in mind that interesting food rewards, such as cheese, liver, chicken, beef jerky, tortellini, hot dogs, roast beef, and steak, or toy rewards, like stuffed animals, tug toys, and Frisbees, all make great rewards. Game rewards like fetch, tug of war, and Frisbee can help an excitable dog to redirect the energy he would have put into chasing a distraction, by focusing it instead on you. Once your dog has focused on you, you can also reward him by allowing him to chase a distraction, such as a squirrel or a leaf, say hello to a person, play with a group of dogs off leash nearby, swim in a pond, plow through the snow, roll in a smell, or whatever else he finds exciting.

Short and Sweet

The best way to use a nonfood reward, such as a game, is to limit the time you interact with the dog after the click to a few seconds. You can also use the real-life reward at the end of the session, as a way to reinforce to the dog that coming to you is a really terrific thing.

Leadership Matters

Ninety percent of a dog's recall has to do with who's in charge. Dogs with firm, strong leaders almost always come when called because they recognize that you are in charge of everything great and your judgment is worth trusting. Remember what it means to be a good leader: It in no way implies being a bully or making your dog do something; in fact, true leaders never have to force a dog to do anything. Leadership is about setting limits and creating rules for what is allowed and what is not allowed.

Having guidelines is essential if your dog is going to do as you wish.

Quite simply, a strong leader controls resources that the dog wants access to, like his dinner, the outdoors, attention and affection, and space, including sleeping places. (Review the guidelines for being a good leader in Chapter 1.) In a nutshell, leadership entails being first, being more powerful, and being in charge. Your ideas and decisions rule, not the dog's. When you give your dog a command, pick the number of seconds that you'll give your dog to respond. Then, if he doesn't respond on the first command within the time frame you've chosen, he doesn't get whatever you were about to give him.

Ready to Reward
Don't miss opportunities to reward your dog for good behavior. Even if you are not directly training your dog to Come, reward your dog for any amount of checking in with you. This in and of itself is sometimes enough to get good check-in behavior started.

You, as the leader, can control what your dog wants by controlling his options and what he's allowed to have. The rule is that when you are experiencing behavior problems, you need to be stricter about allowing privileges and enforcing house rules. Then, when your dog behaves in a more acceptable manner after a few months' time, you can relax some of the rules here and there without losing your status as leader. Think of it as similar to allowing a child to stay up later in the summertime. Staying up later in the summer is a special thing for a child; then, once school rolls around again in September, she knows she will have to go to bed at the usual time.

Building a Foundation for Come

The Come command is really a Leave It command, because the dog has to turn away from what she wants and come back to you. The foundation for Come is the most important part of the exercise. It requires your dog to turn away from the distraction and look back at you (and eventually move toward you as well). The more reliable your dog is about turning away from the things she wants, the better able you will be to get her to come to you any time, any place. If you teach a strong foundation for self-control (see Chapter 4), Come will be easier to train, and your dog will be reliable anywhere you take her. Although you have already taught Come to your dog (also in Chapter 4), take a moment to review the shaping steps again:

1. Stand with your dog on a leash and don't let her get to what she wants; when your dog turns away from what she wants and looks back at you, click and treat.

2. If it takes your dog more than a minute to look back, you are too close to the distraction; back away.

3. When the dog is turning in your direction easily, run backward as she turns to look at you and let her catch you. Click your dog as she is moving toward you and put the treat at your feet.

4. Practice putting the treat between your feet, so when she takes it, it will be easier for you to catch her.

5. Practice handling your dog's collar and leading her by it, clicking and treating her for tolerating your doing so.

6. Label the behavior Come once you have the dog by the collar.

7. Change the environment and distractions, practicing in various places.

8. Use a longer leash, twelve to twenty-five feet, and repeat from the beginning.
9. Let your leash drag until your dog proves she understands the command.
10. Vary the size and type of rewards to keep the dog guessing about what she'll get.

Change old Patterns

Old habits die hard, and a dog who consistently runs away to entertain himself is practicing the very opposite of the behavior you are trying to teach him. If your dog has run away a lot in the past and has gotten away with rewarding himself again and again, you are going to have to put in a lot of time and extra hard work to prevent him from running away.

When your dog refuses to come to you because she has learned that nothing good happens when she does, try to change this setup. For example, call her several times before you actually need to leave and allow her to go back to playing as the reward. Changing *your* pattern of behavior (calling the dog and putting her back on leash, for instance) might be harder than you think, so once again, make sure you have a plan of action that will make training easier. Think ahead about some situations where you can call your dog and then allow her to go back to whatever she is doing once she comes to you, and eventually you will find that your dog is far more likely to come to you than run away.

Keep Recall Positive

Punishment is especially ineffective when teaching your dog to come to you. By the time you're able to punish your dog for running away, you already have him back. In his mind, you are punishing him for coming to you, making it all the more unlikely that he'll respond enthusiastically in the future.

Remote punishment through the use of electronic collars is also not appropriate in the hands of the average pet owner. Even when used by professionals, such devices can teach the dog to be distrustful and fearful of her environment. It is much safer and more reasonable to teach your dog what you expect of her and avoid punishment altogether. Bear in mind that when it comes right down to it, punishment misses the point; it is almost always issued too late to be instructive and if it isn't delivered with perfect timing, it will have absolutely no positive effect on the dog's behavior. Use your time and energy wisely—teach your dog what is expected of her instead of punishing her for making a mistake.

The Critical Link

Just as with every other behavioral problem, exercise is critical for teaching your dog to come to you properly. This point simply cannot be stressed enough. If there is an easy way to put a dent in the solving of a behavior problem, this is it. Almost any professional dog trainer will tell you that a tired dog is a good dog! The more exercise your dog gets, the more likely he will be to come back when you call him. A dog with no opportunity to run and explore will be less likely to return to you on demand. Make sure your dog gets enough time to run around every day. Ideally, he should exercise and wrestle with other dogs, but if interactive play isn't possible, chasing a ball, swimming, or other energy-expending pursuits are a must.

All in the Family

Consider this: The more time you spend exercising your dog, the better you'll feel, too! All levels of the relationship between family and pet benefit from the time you all spend doing things together.

Backyard confinement doesn't count. Most dogs don't want to be by themselves, and without a companion they will often bark, howl, chew, and escape the confines of their yard. Meaningful interaction is the key to engaging the dog's mind and body and making sure that his needs for exercise are met.

Play hide-and-seek with your entire family and take turns letting your dog find you. Call him back and forth to you in the yard, in a big field, or at the beach (have him drag a long leash if you think he'll take off). Play fetch, blow bubbles for him to chase and catch, or take him swimming. Whatever activities you choose, get out, get active, and enjoy your dog and the great outdoors. You'll quickly find that providing more exercise makes your dog more likely to stay closer to you whenever you're out and about.

Safe Confinement

You can confine your dog any number of ways, but it's important to pay careful attention to details so that she can't escape. Keep in mind that no dog should be left unsupervised outdoors unless you have an absolutely escape-proof, locked, chain-link run. You can call a fence company to come and design a dog pen to fit your needs, but don't forget that dogs who are confined outdoors too much tend to develop barking problems.

If you build your own pen, there are several things to think about during design and construction. Ideally, as mentioned in the previous chapter, you should bury ¼-inch mesh wire about three to four inches under a gravel base; that way if your dog decides to dig, she can't dig out. Watch your dog carefully to make sure she doesn't eat the gravel. There are several options you can consider for the bottom surface of the pen. A cement slab might be a good choice if there is adequate shade, but it is not the most comfortable surface to lie on in extreme weather conditions (either hot or cold).

One very effective solution is concrete patio block (or pavers) surrounded by crushed stone. The stones can be whatever size you think will be best for your dog.

Quick Fix: Smooth Car Rides

As soon as your puppy is large enough, start teaching him about riding in the car. Train him to enter and exit the car properly by leashing him, walking him up to the car, and telling him to go in as you give him a boost. Then coax him out of the car by calling "Come" as you gently tug the leash. Practice several times a day, until he goes in and out on command.

Even before your puppy is ready for that lesson, decide where in the car you'd like him to sit. Crating is the safest option in the car, but if this isn't feasible, try a doggy seatbelt, which is available at many pet shops or by mail order. Keeping your dog in one place while riding will ensure good traveling manners, which are essential for the safety of both driver and dog. If your dog jumps around in the car, it can obstruct your view while driving, and that, along with barking or whining, can be extremely distracting and dangerous. Also, a dog who sticks his head out the window can sustain eye injuries, and if you swerve or brake abruptly, he might seriously injure himself.

Depending on the size of your dog pen, you could put some kind of doghouse or shelter at one end; use patio blocks for half the length, and leave the rest of the area with just plain stone. This arrangement makes it easier to disinfect the pen, keeps the smell to a minimum, and is attractive to look at. A locked gate is essential to prevent anyone from stealing your dog. It is really not a good idea to leave your dog unattended, but in circumstances where you need to be gone for an extended period, a pen will at least give your dog a chance to relieve himself in an appropriate place.

Invisible Fences

With an invisible fence, wire is buried around the perimeter of your property, providing an electrical barrier that prevents your dog from leaving the yard. To keep your dog within the confines of the yard, she wears a collar that delivers an electrical correction if she crosses the barrier. Invisible fencing lets you restrict your dog's access to certain areas, like swimming pools, driveways, or decorative gardens. The biggest drawback with these fences, however, is that they do not prevent people or animals from coming onto your property, which is why you should never leave your dog unsupervised in an invisibly fenced area.

In order for this kind of fencing to be used humanely, your dog must be taught to respect the barrier. Hire a qualified professional dog trainer to help you teach your dog where the boundaries are and how to avoid getting corrected.

Although this book promotes positive training methods, if someone can't afford to fence their yard properly, an invisible fence is much better than doing nothing at all. Not using preventative measures increases the risk of your dog getting lost or killed. Keep in mind that some dogs are not bothered by the electrical correction and will run through it. A physical barrier in the form of chain link or solid wood is a much better choice for dogs like these.

Front-Door Safety

Making sure your dog doesn't slip out the front door is essential to keeping her safe. Try to prevent your dog from bolting by thinking ahead and perhaps denying access to the door through which she is most likely to escape. Tighten your screen door so that it closes more quickly, or put a baby gate that locks in the doorway to prevent escapes. Teach your children to be mindful of where the dog is when they are coming and going. Put your dog in a crate or gated room when there are a lot of kids and adults coming and going. Family parties and holiday gatherings are notorious times for dogs to run off and get hit by cars. When you have less control of the home environment, pay special attention to your dog's environment; prevention is always half the cure.

Also spend some time teaching your dog appropriate door manners, like sitting and staying without going through the door (even if it's wide open) until told to do so. This requires lots of on-leash setups with a helper to hold the leash in case your dog tries to make a break. At first, you'll want to practice with the door shut; then gradually build up to your dog holding the Stay while you open and close the door. You can even increase the difficulty by actually going through the door and leaving the dog in a Stay. The key point to remember here is to reinforce the dog for holding the Stay, not coming through the door. Make sure you practice often and provide a high rate of reinforcement for the right behavior.

Teaching your dog reliable recall is probably a more complicated task than you ever imagined. It is not strictly a training issue, but a relationship and management issue as well. Remember that building a strong foundation for Come is essential to getting your dog to realize that you are worth paying attention to, even in a new and exciting environment. Once you have accomplished this reliably, your job will be to anticipate all sorts of variables and then teach your dog to perform the basic task of looking back at you whatever the distractions. In addition to investing the time it will take to teach your dog a reliable recall, take the steps necessary to create a safe and limited environment that he can enjoy.

11: Correcting Other Common Problems

By now, you've learned a lot about controlling many of the major behavior problems dogs often have. You're ready to follow through with housebreaking and proper leash etiquette, and you also know how to discourage digging, barking, and jumping. But what good does this do if you can't even get the leash on without your hyperactive little fur ball sinking her teeth into you? If you're dealing with a young, unruly puppy, there are several other common behavioral issues you need to be prepared for. You probably thought puppy hood would be full of Kodak moments—the kids happily playing ball with the puppy, the puppy curled up asleep in Dad's lap while he watches TV . . . instead, you've got a miniature terrorist on your hands. In the beginning, it might very well seem like all your puppy does is get into or cause trouble.

If you're going nuts because he plays too rough with your kids, cries and whines too often, and makes a speedway out of your home, keep one thing in mind: A puppy is a puppy, and there's no getting around that. Does that mean you just have to grin and bear this trying time? Of course not. But it does mean you need to look at and understand your puppy for what he is: a baby learning about the world. Like human babies, puppies explore with their mouths, their paws (hands), and all their senses. They are soaking up everything about their environment, including how their litter-mates and the "adults" in their world respond to it. If something's exciting to others in their pack, it's sure to be exciting to your puppy; if something smells good, tastes good, or feels good, he wants a part of it, too.

So what are you going to do about it? Like any good parent, your job is to define the rules clearly for your puppy. Not by yelling or punishing your pup—which only makes him afraid of you—but by truly teaching. Knowing what you want your puppy to do is the first step. Then set up small but achievable goals that you and your puppy can celebrate together.

For starters, review the basic training methods described in previous chapters. If your puppy knows how to listen to you when you ask him to Sit, Lie Down, Come, and so on, she'll be more responsive to your teaching when it comes time for solving problem behaviors.

▶ **Welsh Terrier getting into the garbage**

Dog Training Faux Pas

Even the most conscientious, loving dog owners sometimes inadvertently teach their dogs bad behavior. Scan the following list of most common mistakes and see if you're guilty of any:

- Making a big deal out of the arrival of a guest promotes hyper-excited greetings from your dog.
- Feeding your pup while you're cooking, eating, or snacking encourages begging and possessiveness, and it can also cause an upset stomach.
- Throwing strong-smelling items in the wastebasket or leaving trash around can easily instigate garbage raiding (remember, a dog's sense of smell is much keener than ours).
- Leaving clothing, children's toys, and linens hanging around encourages stealing.
- Repeating commands over and over only teaches dogs to ignore them.

Mouthing and Nipping

This is one of the first problems you're apt to encounter with your pup. You probably learned from day one with her that she explores everything with her mouth. This is completely natural; she can't help it! If your puppy came from a sizeable litter, she learned to roughhouse and play with her littermates by using her mouth, body, and paws. She has learned that her mouth is her direct access to everything pleasurable, and also her method for saying, "I've had enough" or "Back off."

Your job is discouraging your puppy from using her mouth to "maul" you or anyone with the sharpness of her teeth or the strength of her jaws. Here's how.

If your puppy chomps down too hard on your finger, hand, wrist, ankle—or any body part—immediately let him know you're in pain. Say, "OUCH" like you really mean it, but don't raise your voice in anger. Never strike out at your puppy, and don't shake your limb or pull it away from your puppy's mouth. Just letting out that yelp should surprise him enough to make him stop pressing down and look up at you.

As soon as your puppy releases you, change your tone completely, and warmly (but *not excitedly*) praise your puppy. Hopefully, you'll have a toy available nearby to give him, so that you can tell him what a good puppy he is when he takes it. When instructed this way, most puppies quickly learn bite inhibition.

 Quick Fix: Manage Mouthing
Puppies teethe from about three to six months of age, and during this time, mouthing and nipping is especially common. As natural as this might be, you must stop mouthing of flesh and valuables regardless of when it occurs, so that it doesn't become habitual. One good way to relieve puppies' teething problems is giving them washcloths that you've wetted, wrung out, and frozen. Chewing on these is great for relieving the discomfort of teething. Just replace with a fresh one when it begins to thaw.

The biggest problem with having a mouthy puppy in the family is that although you might be able to control yourself and respond correctly when puppy gets you with those razor-sharp teeth, it's usually tough for children to respond that way. Their natural tendency is to pull away or flail at the puppy—both of which might encourage the puppy to increase his attempts at nipping because he will mistake these responses for rough play.

Teach your children how to react to this situation by staging it with your puppy and demonstrating the proper response. This way, your puppy and your children will learn at the same time.

Crying and Whining

Believe it or not, these two behaviors are often more bothersome than barking. Why? It's especially difficult for your puppy to understand what you want him to stop doing when he's worked up because of crying or whining. The best remedy is to completely ignore your complaining pup when he's doing either of these things. Admittedly, this is a very difficult task. After all, a crying pup is like a crying baby—your instincts tell you to go to her and do what you can to relieve her discomfort. Remember, however, that dogs will do things to get what they want. If your dog has been adequately fed, exercised, and loved, the only other thing she could possibly want is more attention, more food, or more exercise. But she's not the one who knows best where those things are concerned. If you give in every time your puppy cries or whines, the next thing you know, she might decide she wants to stroll the block at 3 A.M. Even though crying and whining will tug at your heartstrings, remember that you have been responsibly tending to your dog's needs. Crying and whining is just a gimmick to get your attention. Don't become a slave to this tactic!

Be ready, however, to click and reward your puppy the second he stops crying (don't worry—eventually he *will* stop). Give him attention, exercise, a treat, or whatever else to show him he has performed the appropriate behavior. If you're trying to quiet a habitual crier or whiner, be ready to increase the time between when your dog stops and when you go to him, so that he truly recognizes that he's being praised for being quiet.

Playing Too Rough

Many dogs love to play tug of war. It can be a lot of fun for many owners, too—until your fifteen-pound fluff ball grows into a seventy-pound, muscle-bound adolescent who will do anything to win. Or starts to growl whenever you come near any of his toys. This doesn't mean you can't play tug of war. It just means that, as with everything else in dog training, you need to call the shots. You determine when the game begins and when it ends. This is where "Drop It" comes in handy. When tug of war starts to turn into a full-blown battle, immediately say, "Drop It" and stop pulling. If he doesn't let go right away, don't pull again. Say, "Drop It" again. Get up and walk away. Don't turn his resilience into a contest of wills. When your dog has dropped the toy, without saying anything, grab it and put it away where he can't reach or find it by himself.

The same goes for any sort of roughhousing. If your dog gets too out of control, calmly stop whatever you are doing and show him when enough is enough. Keep your play sessions short and in control from the very beginning, and you and your dog will be able to enjoy them within appropriate limits. Make sure the rest of your family understands the game rules, too.

Beware of Biting

Biting should always be considered a serious behavior problem. Whether it occurs because a dog is trying to get our attention, relieve frustration, or change our behavior, biting is never cute, and it's rarely justifiable. Most biting and aggression can be avoided with proper supervision, socialization, training, and intervention by an owner who knows how to recognize the warning signs quickly to stop inappropriate behavior. The signs of impending dog aggression include hard eye contact, stiffening, weight shifting forward, tail out, growling, fast whining, or signs of interest, excitement, or arousal. Whether dealing with playful, fear-driven, or dominant aggression, excellent obedience skills are imperative.

The good news is that aggressive tendencies always diminish as owners' training mastery increases. Through obedience training, owners have the opportunity to learn how to interpret their dog's mood and body language. And an astute observation is often what enables owners to regain control of a potentially aggressive dog well before he reaches a highly agitated state.

Quick Fix: Leave a Bitter Taste

Puppies are master mischief makers, and even if you're diligent about crating your puppy properly and watching her like a hawk when she's loose around the house, there's still a good chance she'll find ways to get into things she shouldn't. If you're concerned that your puppy is tempted to gnaw at the woodwork or bite electrical cords, consider using Bitter Apple spray on the surfaces in question. Bitter Apple doesn't harm wood or furniture, it's nontoxic and biodegradable, and it doesn't irritate the dog's skin. It's also an effective tool for preventing an injured dog from chewing off bandages. (One word of caution—Bitter Apple can harm your dog's eyes, so be careful when spraying.) Wherever you use Bitter Apple, be sure to reapply regularly, because the effects wear off in a day or two. Also, make sure you still keep a close eye on your dog, even after using Bitter Apple, because some dogs actually like the taste!

Submissive Urination

If your dog wets when he greets people or is corrected, he isn't having housebreaking problems. Uncontrollable and unconscious leaking of urine is common in puppies and certain breeds. If your dog has been given a clean bill of health by a veterinarian, stop this tendency by:

- Teaching your dog behavioral commands so she will learn to focus on her responsibilities instead of her emotions.
- Keeping your dog leashed to enable you to prevent misbehavior in a silent, nonemotional manner.
- Avoiding eye contact, talking, and touching during emotional states.
- Keeping your entrances and departures fuss-free.
- Never yelling, striking, or showing anger toward your dog (this should never be done under any circumstances).

Separation Anxiety

Having to leave a dog alone is worrisome if he gets frantically frustrated when he's separated from his owner. Overly dependent dogs commonly respond to separations by continually barking, whining, and howling, destroying living space, and attempting to escape by chewing, digging, and jumping over fences. In addition to causing expensive damage, many dogs, in their extreme panic, also injure themselves. You've probably already guessed that the best way to deal with a dog suffering from separation anxiety is to avoid after-the-fact corrections, which only serve to increase anxiety. But your first instinct—consoling your anxious pup—is not a good idea either. Though well-meaning, your soothing tones and gentle petting can actually reinforce the neurosis you're trying to cure. Here's what you need to do instead:

- Exercise your puppy vigorously and regularly.

- Improve his ability to handle all sources of stress by teaching reliable obedience.
- Remain relaxed as you come and go, and refrain from addressing your dog at those times.

To directly increase your dog's tolerance for separation, practice these exercises:

1. Random tie outs: Teach your dog to remain quiet when you are away from him by taking him to a variety of indoor and outdoor areas, familiar and unfamiliar, filled with or absent of distractions. Silently tie his leash short to a stationary object and walk away for a few minutes. Sometimes remain in sight and other times walk out of sight. When you do return to him, praise him for being a good puppy. Practice frequently, until he is able to stay calm and silent regardless of where you leave him, where you go, and how long you're gone.

2. Out-of-sight Sit- and Down-Stays: This is the same principle as the previous exercise, except you're asking your puppy to stay sitting or lying down as you walk away for increasing amounts of time. However, don't expect a puppy younger than six months old to be able to do these things for longer than a minute or so. Over time, when you work with your puppy on the out-of-sight exercise, you might also get in an occasional Sit-Stay or Down-Stay; whenever this happens, make sure to click and treat him generously, to reward him for doing so. As your puppy gets older, you can increase the lengths of time you ask him to stay seated or down.

Separation problems can periodically return despite these precautions, so be ready to continue to work on the problem, as needed.

Begging

Many times, it only takes one tidbit for your clever puppy to become convinced that your meals are better than hers—and that you're willing to share if she begs. If you've fostered this bad habit, it can be broken, but it's tough to cure. You have to stop feeding your dog ANY human food around mealtime. Sure, your dog is your best buddy, and if you've enjoyed your pizza you probably want to give him some of the crust, because you know it will make him really happy. Be aware of the repercussions, however. Don't expect your dog to differentiate between the times when you casually eat a pizza in front of the TV and gladly share with him, and the time you have your daughter's soccer team over for pizza. In that case, you certainly don't want him underfoot or being fed by every member of the team, because he's sure to get sick!

Distinguish your mealtimes from his by confining him in his crate or a separate room where he can't watch you while you eat. Give him a favorite toy so he's distracted and doesn't whine, cry, drool, or stare you down. Stay strong!

Chewing

The table. The chairs. The rug. The sofa. The car seats. The kids' toys. The garden hose. The swimming pool cover. The TV remote control. A cell phone. You name it and your dog has chewed it to bits. Is there anything worse than that feeling of dread when you come home to find your beloved pooch sound asleep amid a cyclone of destruction? You feed him, exercise him, buy him great toys, give him a comfy bed, keep him healthy, and love him to pieces—and this is what you get in return.

You probably don't want to be reminded of this, but most of the time the destruction is your fault. Remember that section about not

allowing your puppy to have too much freedom too soon, especially
if she is alone in the house? This is precisely why. Maybe you didn't
give her enough puppy-friendly chew toys to keep her occupied,
and you left her alone for too long. Or maybe you just forgot to put
away one of your favorite "things" (handbags and shoes probably
come painfully to mind here) and left it within reach of your inquisi-
tive puppy. Next thing you know, your stuff's history. Whatever the
case, *never* underestimate the reach of a bored puppy.

Quick Fix: The Right Stuff

Be aware that giving your dog certain items can lead to
problems with inappropriate chewing. Avoid giving your
puppy personal items to chew on, such as slippers,
socks, gloves, or towels, because he will not be able to
differentiate between the items that are his and the off-
limit items that belong to you. If your puppy is attracted to
the family's plush toys, don't allow him soft dog toys that
are stuffed or made of fleece. And if he's attracted to
rugs or tassels, never give him rope- or rag-like toys.

When this happens, forget about flying off the handle or punishing your puppy. For your sake and hers, the first and best thing
to do is take your puppy outside. For starters, she's probably in
dire need of relieving herself after all the crazy stuff she's con-
sumed. Survey the damage your pup has done, and make sure
immediately that she hasn't eaten anything that could be poiso-
nous, such as prescription drugs, household cleaners, or house-
plants. (There are many common plants, including azaleas,
poinsettias, and daffodils, that can be toxic to your dog. For more
information and a complete listing, go to *www.aspca.org*, and view
details from the ASPCA's Animal Poison Control Center online.)
Also look to be sure that she hasn't ingested any items that could

be damaging to sensitive body parts, such as pins, splintered bones, or large buttons. If you spot any remnants of dangerous debris, call your veterinarian immediately and ask him or her if you need to bring your puppy in for an examination.

After a thorough investigation, if you find that your pup has emerged unscathed, and it's just your house that's damaged, bring him inside and put him in his crate. Even if you're on the verge of crying or cursing at your dog, refrain from directing your anger toward him. He'll pick up on how upset you are, and if he thinks he's the cause, he might worry that you will always react to him this way. Then all you have is a puppy who hasn't learned anything other than Mommy and Daddy are scary when they come home. This will only make your puppy more anxious, which will lead to more destructive chewing.

Stay as calm as possible when mishaps like this occur, and instead work on preventing future recurrences. Take some tips for fun, interesting chew toys that will hold your dog's attention from those mentioned in previous chapters, such as rubber Kongs smeared with peanut butter or pig's ears with cream cheese.

Food for Thought
Edible products such as rawhide, pig's ears, and cow hoofs can be great rewards, snacks, or chew toys for your dog, but be careful about giving them to young puppies. These things can increase your puppy's thirst, can possibly upset his stomach, or even get lodged in his intestines, prompting a medical emergency. Some puppies also get defensive and possessive around edible items. If your puppy is having house-soiling problems or gets tense in the presence of these edible items, get rid of them. If you're unsure or concerned about side effects, consult your breeder or veterinarian.

Stealing and Scavenging

If you were left all alone in someone else's house, wouldn't you get bored and look for diversions? Now you know how your dog feels. Except when she's trapped and bored, she can't read or raid the refrigerator. But she does have plenty of senses yearning to be indulged. For this reason, many dogs snatch things for their own amusement while you're not home. Just like chewing, when your dog is given too much freedom too soon, she will quickly discover the joys of hunting for household treasures left easily accessible by negligent humans. Dogs know that one of the best ways to rouse you from your recliner is to show off the loot they've confiscated.

In order to prevent this type of behavior, it's crucial to be consistent with crating. Even when you are at home, keep your eyes glued on your little bandit constantly. Don't be a victim of your dog's shenanigans—think about prevention and strategic placement. Keep the garbage out of reach, pick up toys, close cabinets and closets, and put laundry away. Teach your dog "Drop It" and "Leave It," and dispense justice fairly. Only interrupt crimes in progress, never correct or punish stealing after the fact. When you catch your dog in the act, redirect his attention to something more appropriate, such as a toy. Then, when he does something more appropriate, click him and give him a reward.

When dealing with any of these common problems, remember that prevention is always the best strategy. Giving an untrained dog unrestricted freedom throughout the house is not only damaging, it can be deadly. Puppies are naturally curious, and this can prompt them to chew on electrical cords, ingest toxic substances, or get into dangerous places. Don't forget—puppies are opportunists. We are the foolish ones if we walk out of a room and leave a young, untrained dog to do as she pleases without any supervision to keep her safe and out of mischief.

12: Coping with Fears and Phobias

Do you have a dog who is a sweet, wonderful family pet in familiar surroundings, but turns into a mess of jittery shaking nerves in new places where he encounters strange sounds and unfamiliar people? Without a doubt, a fearful dog can be a challenge to train. If you own a dog like this, it is important to educate yourself and learn all you can in order to help your dog become a less afraid and more confident companion.

All in a Day's Work

Depending on your dog's breed and personality, she might need more social experience than average. Working and herding breeds are notoriously more suspicious of new people and things. They are bred to notice what is different and to react to it, which is what makes them so good at herding and guarding. No wonder they need more socialization than the average dog to differentiate between friend and foe. If you have a dog such as this, expose her to as many good experiences as possible, so that she will overcome her apprehension and suspicion and accept new people and things as a normal part of her world.

Phobic dogs are a mix of unfortunate experiences and a lack of early socialization appropriate for their temperament. Retraining these dogs to be more secure can be a challenge, but fearful dogs don't have to stay that way forever. With lots of patience and careful training, you can help your dog enjoy life a lot more. Keep in mind that building confidence in a fearful dog is time consuming; don't expect miracles overnight. Be flexible in your plan, allow for regression, and figure out how you will handle it. Being prepared for setbacks will help your dog to gain assurance more quickly. If you panic or flounder when things don't go as planned, it will only confuse your dog. But if you, as her handler, remain confident, shift plans, and continue, she will feel assured, too.

Making a Commitment to Training

Fearful dogs do not suddenly become confident, even with lots of training. Training a fearful dog to be more confident is a time-consuming project. The best approach is having a determined attitude and setting clear, achievable goals. Being specific about how you want your dog to react and behave is particularly important in the case of an apprehensive dog.

When training a fearful dog it is important to adapt; keep in mind that you will not always progress as consistently as you would like. Be flexible enough to realize when you've pushed too hard and insightful enough to know what changes to make so that your dog will be successful. These are two of the most important elements of a good dog trainer.

Be organized and Consistent

Having a regular schedule is absolutely critical when working with a dog who is fearful. Breaking your goals down into steps is the key to seeing improvement in a relatively short period of time. For instance, teaching your dog to make a game out of what she is afraid of, through targeting, is a great way to build her confidence. If you practice targeting enough, it will become second nature to your dog and she will learn to play the game regardless of what else is going on around her.

Maybe your dog is afraid of strange men, for example. You might start off by using a male member of your family whom your dog likes and teaching her to target the person's hand.

Teaching a fearful dog to approach a strange person and touch her nose to his hand probably won't be easy. This task would need to be broken down into really tiny pieces if the dog is particularly afraid of the strange person. For instance, you might want to have the person sit in a chair and ignore the dog at first. Then, you could have the stranger drop small pieces of treats around their feet and let your dog take her time eating them. If your dog is too scared to eat, break it down into something even easier, like having the person lie on the couch or sit a greater distance away. Your dog's appetite is a good indicator of her comfort level. If she is too stressed to eat, you need to make changes to make progress.

In this example, after the dog relaxes enough to eat the treats, you would gradually change the variables so that eventually the dog is able to target the person's hand for a click and treat.

Just don't jump right into targeting with strange people. Most people who have been successful using this method to help their dogs overcome their anxiety have worked with their dogs extensively, first to teach them to target their own hands and then the hands of people the dog likes. Once you've built up your dog's confidence around familiar people, targeting can then be used to teach your dog to be brave around new people and other scary things.

Taking the time to teach your dog how to target will be one of the most important training tools you have to help your dog get over his fears. Once you do, you will find that because targeting creates such positive associations for your dog, he will be more willing to extend himself and be open to new experiences. Targeting is a wonderful technique, because it will give your dog something constructive to do instead of being scared.

Fierce or Fearful Dogs

Aggression and fearfulness are two behavior problems that are stressful for both dog and handler. Keeping your dog from getting too overwhelmed and getting his attention back on you is your primary goal as the owner of a fearful or aggressive dog. You want to help your dog to associate the things he is afraid of with positive reinforcement. There's no better way to do that than to teach him constructive behavior alternatives in instances where he normally reacts aggressively or fearfully. Teach him to look at you for an extended period of time, to touch your hand with his nose, to touch an object, or another person's hand. Just remember to build up to these things slowly.

Genetics, Abuse, or a Lack of Exposure?

People often assume that fearful dogs have been mistreated by a prior owner or some other person who has had contact with the dog. More commonly, dogs are fearful or phobic because they lacked early exposure to different types of people, sounds, and experiences, including other dogs. Genetics can also play a large role in shaping a dog's fearful behavior, and some breeds have shyness as a common, though undesirable, trait. Remember, however, that even though certain types of dogs might be more prone to fearfulness, *any* dog can grow up being fearful and suspicious due to negative experiences or lack of proper training early in life.

A Reputable Source

It is very important to research who you are buying your puppy from. Steer clear of puppy mills, pet stores, and other places where they raise more than one breed.

Breeding

A good breeder is committed to turning out puppies who are healthy, well adjusted, and ready for life. They screen their puppies' potential owners and educate each person who buys a puppy about how to train and socialize their puppies appropriately. You get what you pay for, and quality puppies from good breeders don't come cheap. A lot of love and care goes into each puppy if the breeder does his or her job right.

If you feel your dog's problems stem from a genetic component, it is still possible to train her. Even in well-bred dogs with conscientious breeders, some puppies can be more fearful than their littermates. If this natural shyness is identified early enough, and intensive socialization and training is implemented, progress can be made in a short period of time, even with timid pups.

Determining Puppy Personality

The puppy aptitude test is a series of tests performed on forty-nine-day-old puppies that helps determine their tendencies to be outgoing, shy, mischievous, or pushy. More information on puppy aptitude testing can also be obtained from DogWise, a dog and cat book retailer, which can be found online at ✍www.dogwise.com.

A genetic predisposition to noise sensitivity is common in many breeds used for hunting and sporting purposes. Dog breeders who truly care will breed out these traits by choosing only the friendliest, most confident dogs for their breeding programs. If you are looking for a puppy of a breed that has fearful tendencies, ask questions about the parents' temperaments, meet both parents, and choose a breeder who has someone perform the puppy aptitude test on all of their litters. (Developed by dog trainers Wendy and Joachim Volhard, the puppy aptitude test is a widely used method for selecting the proper puppy for the right home. Go to *www.volhard.com* for a printer-friendly version.) Dogs who are carefully bred by knowledgeable, concerned people should be friendly and outgoing regardless of their breed.

Social Development

If you feel your dog's fearfulness is a result of lack of early socialization, and your dog is still under a year old, get out there and get busy. The earlier you start to change this, the more successful your training program will be. The longer you wait, the harder it will be to change these tendencies.

In this case, it is particularly important to enroll your dog in a well-organized group training class. Be honest with your instructor about what your goals are, and ask if a group class would be an appropriate place to start with your dog. Also, if you're considering a doggie day care facility, talk to the staff about your dog's apprehension. There are doggie day cares that take on special cases, and often the staff is very knowledgeable about these problems. They can help make sure your dog learns to overcome his fears and has an enjoyable experience.

Getting a puppy from a person who has been raising dogs for many years and knows how to provide the right kind of environment will save you a lot of problems in the long run. If a puppy misses out on these critical early social periods and is not raised in an environment that stimulates him to explore and learn about his world, he will be a fearful, phobic adult dog.

While shyness, fear, and fear-related aggression are sometimes the result of lack of socialization, there are dogs out there who have been mistreated and are fearful and skittish as a result of learning that strange people and places are scary and dangerous. Naturally, these dogs need love and attention to help them to learn to trust people, but making excuses for or trying to coddle them will not fix the problem. It might actually make it worse. The same basic advice applies for teaching dogs who have been mistreated. Remedial socialization (socializing a dog after the optimum age of eight to eighteen weeks) is time consuming and fraught with regression and frustration, but ultimately, it's well worth the effort.

▶ **Two Welch Terriers and an Airedale Terrier**

Stair Climbing

If your dog is afraid to go up and down the stairs, you'll need to practice with him. Start on no more than half a flight of stairs and use a very wide stairway with good traction. Leash your dog, grip the railing, and slowly progress up or down one step at a time, looking straight ahead to convey confidence. Expect the first step to be the biggest challenge, and ignore his balking. Rather than allowing him to avoid the stairs, support him by holding his leash short and tight, to prevent him from losing balance. Repeat this training often, and click and treat each time your dog succeeds in climbing a step.

Introduce a young puppy to the stairs by placing him on the bottom stair. Then, either wait for him to gather the courage to jump off, or try to coax him by sitting on the floor with a toy he likes. When he's mastered that step, place him on the second-to-last stair, and then progress one stair at a time from there until he has mastered the entire flight. If a puppy will walk down stairs, usually he'll have no problem going up.

Now Get Busy

All dogs need structure, but fearful dogs need even more. The more predictable the schedule and house rules, the better able they will be to cope with life. Spoiling or indulging these dogs will make matters worse; above all else, a fearful dog needs a strong, fair, and consistent leader. Providing structure for a fearful dog means feeding, walking, and exercising him at specific times. It also means making sure that house rules are rarely broken. For instance, your dog should always sit before you take him outside, put his food dish on the floor, or hook on his leash for a walk.

Whatever they might be, rules are crucial, because a dog who knows what is expected of her will know that someone else is going to take care of her. This alone will give her more confidence. Eventually, house rules can be flexible, but not until your dog is more confident. The stricter and more consistent the rules are, the quicker the dog will be to trust that you can take care of her, and the more she will look to you for leadership.

Establish Rules

There are several things you can do to help raise your dog's confidence level to make training more successful.

Avoid reinforcing fearful behavior. Petting and talking soothingly to the dog or picking him up reinforces fearful behavior. A hands-off approach works better. Calmly telling your dog that everything is fine conveys the message that there is nothing to fear.

No punishment—ever! If a dog is frightened, she is in an emotional state, not a learning state. Physical or verbal correction will only convince her that there really is something to fear. Punishment might even bring out aggression if your dog feels threatened and vulnerable. Avoid any type of correction; it won't solve the problem.

Safety first. Remember that fearful dogs often behave in unexpected ways that can end with them getting hurt. Keep the leash on at all times in public and make all the exits in your house escape-proof. Deny your dog access to the front door, for instance, if she is constantly looking to dash out the door when she panics during thunderstorms or with loud noises.

Exercise and mental stimulation. Dogs who lack confidence need exercise more than ever. Chasing a ball, hide-and-seek, learning tricks, agility, fly ball, or any other sports are excellent ways for your dog to release her daily energy reserves and tension, as she builds courage and self-confidence.

Pay attention to providing the right environment for your dog. Make sure it's one in which she can learn to trust, because it is consistent and predictable. This will put you on the road toward helping your dog to become a more secure and enjoyable companion.

Quick Fix: Carsick Canines

If your dog gets carsick, make sure she associates car riding with pleasant things, not just stressful experiences such as traveling to the vet's office. The more relaxed your dog is about getting in the car, the less inclined she'll be toward motion sickness. Also remember not to feed her for several hours prior to riding. Keeping the car's air temperature comfortably cool helps, too—just make sure that if you roll down a window, your dog can't stick her head out. To further reduce the risk of motion sickness, avoid bumpy roads and abrupt stops or turns. If motion sickness continues to be a problem for your dog, ask your veterinarian about using medication.

Classical Conditioning

Using classical conditioning can help you cover more ground more quickly because rather than requiring your dog to perform a certain behavior, it deals with associations and feelings. Since classical conditioning involves creating the association that "scary thing" equals "good stuff," this technique can be helpful for dogs who are too scared to work at all. It also works well for dogs who have noise sensitivities and other phobias.

Remember that classical conditioning works by opening the

bar each time something that induces fear is present. So as soon as your dog hears a loud noise, for example, toss treats on the ground, throw a ball, or play a favorite game. When the noise goes away, so does all the good stuff. Take away your attention, too, and ignore your dog for at least five minutes. In this way, you should be able to change your dog's association from fear to expecting good things to happen.

Using classical conditioning is a good way to make huge deposits in your dog's bank account for combating fear. Half the problem of training a scared dog is that he is not relaxed enough to absorb the lesson and, therefore, training requires more repetition and more changes of variables. Classical conditioning will complement your dog's operant training program because you'll have a more relaxed dog to train.

Systematic Desensitization

This technique involves playing a noise at a very low volume or keeping a scary person or thing at enough distance so that the dog notices it but does not react fearfully to it. A good rule of thumb is that if your dog won't take a treat or play with you, the volume is too high or the distance is too close. Increase the volume gradually, or bring the person or thing closer, so that eventually the dog will ignore it altogether and continue to take treats and play.

The process of systematic desensitization involves interacting with the dog in a positive way, be it with a game of fetch or teaching tricks, in order to help the dog develop a more positive association with the thing that is feared. The dog starts to associate the feeling of being relaxed around the scary noise or object and eventually the volume can be increased and the distance decreased until the dog will accept the new thing as part of his environment and no longer finds it threatening.

Veterinary Behaviorist and Alternative Solutions

Veterinary behaviorists are skilled both as veterinarians and as dog behavior experts. You might consider consulting a behaviorist to help diagnose your dog's problem and show you how to start working toward a solution. The main difference between a veterinary behaviorist and a dog trainer/behaviorist is that the veterinary behaviorist can prescribe medication for dogs with problems that are too intense or severe to change with training alone.

Quick Fix: Create Some Clamor

If loud noises frighten your dog, making him hard to control, you can also desensitize him to noise by allowing him to create his own racket. Let him bat around a big metal spoon with a little peanut butter on it, or give him an empty milk container with a bit of squeeze cheese in the rim to play with. It won't be long before he is creating a hubbub and loving it. Of course, the clamor could drive you nuts, so think about limiting his playtime with noisemakers!

Consider seeking the help of a veterinary behaviorist if you don't seem to be making any progress over six weeks' time or if your dog seems unnaturally fearful. For instance, dogs who are so fearful of being left alone that they injure themselves or severely destroy their surroundings in their owner's absence might benefit from veterinary-prescribed drugs. Such medications can help to restore a dog's chemical balance and assist them in learning appropriate and alternative behavior. If your dog suffers from a chemical imbalance, no amount of training will change that. Restoring the body to its equilibrium will ensure that your dog will be able to make the most of his training sessions and will make progress faster. In most cases the goal is to wean the dog off the medication by adhering to a strict behavioral program until the dog learns a new response.

Veterinary behaviorists also have experience with difficult or unusual problems, such as severe separation anxiety, aggression, excessive tail chasing, shadow chasing, or other obsessive behaviors. A veterinary behaviorist usually charges a substantial fee, which covers the initial visit. On the first visit, the behaviorist will meet your dog and take a complete history in order to diagnose your dog's problem and advise you on the treatment.

The behaviorist will most likely design a training program for you to follow and require that you give updates on your dog's progress. In some cases the behaviorist might even refer you to a local obedience trainer to coach you as you implement the program. Not all problems require medication, but in some severe cases pharmacological intervention can save you huge amounts of time and make the success of your training program more likely.

Natural Remedies

If training and conditioning are not enough to help your dog, holistic veterinary practitioners, who use alternative solutions to relieve fear and anxiety, are another option. At first it might seem like some of the solutions don't appear to fit your problems. You might not have even considered some treatments, like massage, acupuncture, or a homeopathic remedy. But if you have a dog who has complex behavior problems, it is crucial to keep an open mind about alternative methods of treatment.

Homeopathic remedies often work to help your dog restore his natural balance so that his body can heal itself. If you do decide to go this route, the veterinarian will take a detailed history of not only your dog's heath and diet but also his likes, dislikes, and general behavioral issues.

Consider seeking out a professional to consult with to see what recommendations she might have for your dog. She might use a combination of herbal remedies, body wraps, massage techniques, and behavioral training to help you achieve your goal of a more confident pet. The more alternatives you seek, the more likely you will be to find a solution that will help improve the overall wellness of your dog and the speed of his training program.

Seek Alternatives
To find alternative practitioners like acupuncturists, chiropractors, massage therapists, or other types of specialists in your area, try asking other dog owners, looking in the yellow pages, asking at your local health food store, contacting the nearest veterinary school, or doing a search on the Internet.

other Alternative Solutions
Fear is an emotion that can get in the way of training; because of this, you might find that training alone is not the entire solution. Consider seeking out alternative methods of treatment to be sure you have covered all the bases. Sometimes, fears are the result of an injury or underlying medical problem that goes undetected. Often, however, these problems can be successfully identified through chiropractic or acupuncture consultations.

There are many massage techniques available for dogs, including the Tellington Touch (see Chapter 6). This type of technique helps dogs to become more confident and aware of their bodies and works well in conjunction with a behavior modification program. Regardless of what you start with, the general rule to keep in mind is to do no harm. The more open-minded you are toward trying something new, the more your dog will benefit. If you have a difficult problem, the best approach is to seek as much information as possible so that you have lots of tools to help your dog live the happiest, healthiest, and most comfortable life possible.

13: Advancing Beyond the Basics

By now, hopefully, congratulations are in order, as you have turned your unruly fur ball into a model of good canine behavior. If you've successfully tackled barking, jumping, digging, and leash lunging, and your dog is attentively obedient to basic commands like Heel, Sit, and Stay, you might be ready to try something more advanced.

Obedience Trials

Obedience trialing is a rewarding endeavor that doesn't require extensive travel or a lot of money. Anyone can participate in the sport of dog obedience. Desire is far more important than natural talent. People of all ages and physical conditions can become top competitors, and dogs of all breeds and backgrounds (rescued and formerly abused dogs, too) appear in the winner's circle. Handlers who participate in obedience training will experience the rewards of a better trained dog as well as the camaraderie with peers—and maybe even the thrill of earning an occasional title.

Obedience trials test and score a dog's ability to perform specific exercises. The American Kennel Club sanctions the majority of these events. The AKC has more than 13,000 field trial, obedience, and other specialty clubs, and hundreds of AKC-sanctioned dog shows occur every week all over the United States. Trials governed by the United Kennel Club, States Kennel Club, and others are also quickly gaining popularity. Regardless of which kennel club is governing, the rules are nearly identical, or involve only minor variations, so little additional training is required to earn more titles. In AKC and most other obedience competitions, dogs work toward titles in three levels, each progressively more difficult. The classes, titles, and general summary of requirements are as follows:

Novice—Companion Dog (CD): This level includes on- and off-leash heeling, recall and stand, sit and down stay. Novice is the only class in which the dog is leashed for part of the performance and, when the leash is removed, the handler can guide the dog by the collar while moving from one exercise to the next.

Open—Companion Dog Excellent (CDX): This level involves commands such as drop on recall, retrieve on flat, retrieve over high jump, broad jump, and sit and down stays with the handlers out of sight.

Utility—Utility Dog (UD): This category tests hand signals, scent discrimination, moving stand, and directed jumping and retrieving.

Open and Utility are considered the advanced classes. In these, the leash is removed as the team enters the ring. The dog is never touched, except to be measured or praised. In order to earn a title in each level the dog must earn three qualifying scores. A perfect score is 200 points, and to qualify a dog must earn 170 points and 50 percent of the available points for each exercise.

Dogs who earn a UD are eligible to compete for two other

obedience titles. The UDX (Utility Dog Excellent) is earned when the dog qualifies in Open and Utility class at the same show ten times. The OTCh (Obedience Trial Championship) is won after the dog accumulates 100 points. Points are earned if the dog places first or second in Open or Utility, and the number of points earned is determined by the size of the class. This is the only competitive obedience title, meaning a dog earns points by defeating other dogs, rather than simply performing exercises in accordance with the rulebook. Special competitions, otherwise known as tournaments, are held for the best of the best. In order to enter, the dog must prove himself at AKC or other kennel-club sanctioned events. Top obedience dogs are ranked each year using various systems designed by breed clubs, obedience clubs, and obedience publications such as *Front and Finish*, or *The Dog Trainer's News*. Although these aren't official designations, they're esteemed and sought after.

Expanding Your Training Circle

Many competitors hire private instructors either as their sole means of coaching or to supplement group training instruction. Most trialers also gather informally with other trialers to practice working their dogs around distractions. Your canine social circle will quickly expand as you become involved in training classes, seminars, and practice matches. When selecting a private instructor, inquire about the techniques he uses, as well as his personal obedience trial experience and the titles he's earned. Also ask about experience he's had working with your breed. And don't forget to check client referrals. A good rapport with a private instructor is a must. It will help you stay inspired and motivated to work your dog when the going gets tough.

American Kennel Club competitions are limited to purebred registered and ILP (indefinite listing privilege) dogs, but many governing bodies allow mixed breeds to compete. All obedience competitions allow spayed and neutered dogs to participate. If you'd like to observe an obedience trial, call local training clubs or browse dog show superintendents' pages on the Internet. For information, check out the American Kennel Club Web site, at *www.akc.org*, or the United Kennel Club Web site, at *www.ukcdogs.com*. You're likely to find events several times each month that take place within easy driving distance from where you live.

Advanced Exercises

Even if you're not sure you are interested in obedience competition, you should definitely continue training your dog beyond the basics. The following advanced techniques are helpful for competition, but they are also fun to train.

▶ **Two Golden Retrievers and a German Shepherd**

Hand Signals, Whistles, and Snap Commands

It's imperative to use clear, concise, and consistent commands, but verbal commands aren't the only type that fit the bill. For instance, a snap of your fingers followed by a point at the ground can mean lie down—not a bad idea when you're brushing your teeth and you want your dog to stop misbehaving!

Whistles are commonly used in the field because the sound travels so well. Initially though, the dog must be trained close to the handler to understand the association between behaviors and whistles. Generally, one toot of the whistle means sit and stay, and multiple toots mean come into "Heel" position.

Teaching hand signals is easy. Always give your hand signal in a distinct way so your dog can clearly pick up on the movement, and make sure the signal is controlled and precise. Obedience trial regulations allow handlers to use the entire arm and hand in a single motion, but penalize any other body motion. Start by teaching hand signals for basic commands. Whether using a standard verbal command or a nonverbal cue, the process of teaching your dog any task is the same: Give the cue, then click, treat, and praise your dog when he performs the appropriate task.

Fire Away!

Once your dog has mastered basic commands, teach her to obey them in rapid succession. Rapid-fire commands require your dog to focus and give you her undivided attention quickly. Practice by initiating a series of quick commands. Start by commanding "Sit," then release; next, command "Come," run twenty feet away from your dog, and release; follow with "Down," release; then instruct your dog to "Heel" at various speeds, including halts and turns; finally, end with a "Down" command again. That sequence should take fifteen to twenty seconds. When you've mastered the routine, work up to sequences of three to five minutes.

By practicing rapid-fire commands, you'll become a more efficient and effective trainer, and you'll see terrific results in shorter periods of time. Rapid-fire commands are a great way to expend your dog's energy and stimulate her mind. If learned properly, these techniques will greatly improve your dog's reliability and sharpen her obedience skills.

off-Leash Commands

Any dog who is going to continue beyond novice obedience trials needs to learn to follow commands off leash. The concept of off-leash training is a bit of a misnomer, however, because all teaching must first be done on leash. Off-leash activity only reinforces the good work your dog learns to do on-leash. If a dog is not fully prepared on-leash, his lack of understanding will only multiply when the leash comes off, so make sure your dog is totally ready for the transition.

Try this experiment before attempting off-lead work: With your dog dragging her leash, and your arms folded or in your pockets, give a "Sit," "Down," or "Come" command in a nonthreatening voice. That command should be easy for her. Next, choose the strongest temptation for your dog—the doorbell, an open field, or the presence of other people or animals—and try the experiment again. Click, treat, and praise her if she listens—you might be ready at this point to wean your dog off the line. If she doesn't, pick that leash up, because you need to review basic on-lead commands around distractions before attempting off-lead work.

"Straitjacket" Commands

No, this has nothing to do with confining your rambunctious pal; this term applies to you! Be very conscious of your mannerisms when making the transition to off-leash work with your dog. As you were teaching your dog on-lead obedience, you might have used excessive body language or gestures, consciously or unconsciously. But these no longer seem significant when your dog gets further away during off-lead work. It's easy to assume that disobedience occurs because your dog is off leash; in actuality, it's possible that he was never taught to obey your commands without the additional cues.

Practice giving your dog "straightjacket" commands by attaching the leash, folding your arms, or putting your hands in your pockets, then giving "Sit," "Stay," "Come," and other commands. Avoid touching the leash to enforce these commands. Use no gestures, just your voice. After all, at a distance, he'll only hear your voice, and the gestures will be wasted if he is running away.

Whether or not you decide to commit yourself to obedience trialing as an ongoing hobby, it's always a good idea to pursue advanced training. The more you train, the better your control, and the stronger the bond between you and your dog will be.

Canine Well-Wishers

Obedience competition is not the only logical progression beyond basic dog training. As you've learned from past chapters, a well-trained, obedient dog is a joy to take with you anywhere. So now that your dog has made the grade, why not spread some of that joy around? Dogs who are well trained in obedience, have generally sweet dispositions, and love to be with people are often great therapy dogs. These dogs visit hospitals and nursing homes and they make enormous differences in people's lives. There are several organizations that certify dogs for this work. The Delta Society is the largest resource for this type of information. (See Appendix for contacts.) Being a member of a therapy-dog organization will not only provide you with insurance coverage, it will give you the benefit of belonging to an organization that supports and guides the use of animals in hospitals and nursing homes.

Therapy dogs have been helping people to cope with life for decades, and the work they do is varied. The visit might simply involve cuddling or petting, or it might help with something more complicated, such as a speech lesson or physical therapy session. Regardless of the intensity, a visit from a therapy dog can change the course of a patient's treatment. There are countless stories of people talking for the first time or reaching some elusive milestone because of the uplifting and encouraging presence of a dog. Dogs lighten the mood and make the work of rehabilitation in therapy a little less grueling. In nursing homes across the country, dogs take long, lonely, endless days and turn them into something to look forward to. A therapy dog is a dog whose pure intelligence, beauty, and love are put to the best use possible.

Good PR

Consider forming an association of responsible dog owners in your city and petitioning for public open spaces to exercise your dog. Stressing your role as a taxpayer who enjoys the companionship of your dog is essential to gaining access to public spaces. Using a little social peer pressure to get dog-owning neighbors and friends to comply with pooper-scooper laws, leash manners, and overall pet owner responsibility is a giant step toward the acceptance of dogs in public spaces.

Dogs bring such joy to all those around them when they are trained and cared for by the people who love them. By educating yourself and your dog, you are investing back into your enjoyment of your dog and the interactions she has with those around her. Set the example by training your dog well, spread the word, and show the world that owning a dog is an experience that no one should miss.

Appendix

Resources

Books

Abrantes, Roger. *Dog Language: An Encyclopedia of Canine Behavior* (Naperville, IL: Wakan Tanka Publishers, 1997).

Benjamin, Carol. *Dog Problems* (New York, NY: Hungry Minds, Inc., 1989).

Burch, Mary R. and Jon S. Bailey. *How Dogs Learn* (New York, NY: Hungry Minds, Inc., 1999).

Campbell, William E. *Behavior Problems in Dogs*, Third Revised Edition (Grants Pass, OR: BehaviorRx Systems, 1999).

Campbell, William E. *Owner's Guide to Better Behavior in Dogs* (Loveland, CO: Alpine Publishers, 1989).

Cantrell, Krista. *Catch Your Dog Doing Something Right: How to Train Any Dog in Five Minutes a Day* (New York, NY: Plume Publishers, 1998).

Donaldson, Jean. *The Culture Clash* (Berkeley, CA: James and Kenneth Publishing, 1997).

Donaldson, Jean. *Dogs Are from Neptune* (Montreal, Quebec: Lasar Multimedia Productions, 1998).

Dunbar, Ian. *Dr. Dunbar's Good Little Dog Book* (Berkeley, CA: James and Kenneth Publishers, 1992).

Dunbar, Ian. *How to Teach a New Dog Old Tricks* (Berkeley, CA: James and Kenneth Publishers, 1998).

Evans, Job Michael. *Training and Explaining: How to Be the Dog Trainer You Want to Be* (New York, NY: Hungry Minds, Inc., 1995).

Fox, Dr. Michael W. *Understanding Your Dog* (New York, NY: St. Martin's Press, 1972).

Milani, D.V.M., Myrna. *The Body Language and Emotions of Dogs* (New York, NY: William Morrow and Company, 1986).

Milani, D.V.M., Myrna. *DogSmart* (Chicago, IL: Contemporary Publishing, 1997).

Owens, Paul. *The Dog Whisperer: A Compassionate, Nonviolent Approach to Dog Training* (Avon, MA: Adams Media, 1999).

Pryor, Karen. *Don't Shoot the Dog: The New Art of Teaching and Training*, Revised Edition (New York, NY: Bantam Books, 1999).

Pryor, Karen. *Karen Pryor on Behavior: Essays and Research* (North Bend, WA: Sunshine Books, 1994).

Reid, Ph.D., Pamela. *Excel-Erated Learning: Explaining in Plain English How Dogs Learn and How Best to Teach Them* (Oakland, CA: James and Kenneth Publishers, 1996).

Rugaas, Turid. *On Talking Terms with Dogs: Calming Signals* (Carlsborg, WA: Legacy By Mail, 1997).

Ryan, Terry. *The Toolbox for Remodeling Your Problem Dog* (New York, NY: Howell Book House, 1998).

Schwartz, Charlotte. *The Howell Book of Puppy Raising* (New York, NY: Hungry Minds, Inc., 1987).

Scott, John Paul and John L. Fuller. *Genetics and the Social Behavior of the Dog* (Chicago, IL: University of Chicago Press, 1965).

Tellington-Jones, Linda. *Getting in Touch with Your Dog: A Gentle Approach to Influencing Health, Behavior, and Performance* (Pomfret, VT: Trafalgar Square, 2001).

Wilkes, Gary. *A Behavior Sampler* (North Bend, WA: Sunshine

Books, 1994).

Videos

Broitman, Virginia. *Bow Wow, Take 2* (Littleton, CO: Canine Training Systems, 1996).

Broitman, Virginia and Sherry Lippman. *Take a Bow Wow* (Littleton, CO: Canine Training Systems, 1996).

Jones, Deborah. *Click & Fetch* (Littleton, CO: Canine Training Systems, 1999).

Pryor, Karen. *Clicker Magic! The Art of Clicker Training* (North Bend, WA: Sunshine Books, 1997).

Pryor, Karen. *Puppy Love* (North Bend, WA: Sunshine Books, 1999).

Rugaas, Turid. *Calming Signals: What Your Dog Tells You* (Carlsborg, WA: Legacy By Mail, 2001).

Wilkes, Gary. *Click! & Treat Training Kit* (Phoenix, AZ: Click! & Treat Products, 1996).

Wilkes, Gary. *The Doggie Repair Kit* (Phoenix, AZ: Click! & Treat Products, 1996).

organizations

American Kennel Club (AKC)

Phone: 212-696-8200

Web site: *www.akc.org*

American Society for the Prevention of Cruelty to Animals (ASPCA)

Phone: 212-876-7700

Web site: *www.aspca.org*

E-mail: *information@aspca.org*

The Association of Pet Dog Trainers (APDT)

Phone: 800-738-3647

Web site: *www.apdt.com*
E-mail: *information@apdt.com*
Delta Society
Phone: 425-226-7357
Web site: *www.deltasociety.org*
E-mail: *info@deltasociety.org*

Therapy Dogs International
Phone: 973-252-9800
Web site: *www.tdi-dog.org*
E-mail: *tdi@gti.net*

United Kennel Club
Phone: 269-343-9020
Web site: *www.ukcdogs.com*
E-mail: *pbickell@ukcdogs.com* (general registration questions)

Whole-Dog-Journal.com
Phone: 800-829-9165
Web site: *www.whole-dog-journal.com*
E-mail: *WholeDogJ@aol.com*

Web Sites

Canine University®: *www.canineuniversity.com*
DogWise: *www.dogwise.com*
Karen Pryor's Web site: *www.dontshootthedog.com*
William Campbell's Web site: *www.webtrail.com/petbehavior/index.html*

Index

Acknowledgments

Special thanks from Adams Media to all of the dogs who appear throughout this book, and to their human families for supplying us with their photos: Lynda Warwick, Jen Stiles, and Molly; Karen Hocker and Dieffenbaker; Dawn Sullivan, Millie, and Scootchie; Carol Raheily and Max; Peggy McNally, Bo, Haley, and Cassie; and Gerilyn and Paul Bielakiewicz, Reggae and Stryker.